FOOD
TRAILS OF
INDIA

Mrinal Tulpule

Sakāl

Food Trails Of India

© Mrinal Tulpule (2024)

Sakal Media Pvt. Ltd.
595, Budhwar Peth,
Pune – 411002, India
www. sakalmediagroup. com
sakalprakashan@esakal. com

First Edition : Oct 2024

The views expressed in this book are those of the Authors and do not necessarily reflect the views of the Publishers.

Although the Editors and the Authors have made every effort to ensure that the information in this book is correct at the time of printing, the Editors, Authors and the Publishers do not assume and hereby disclaim any liability to any party for any loss, damage, or disruption caused by errors or omissions, whether such errors or omissions result from negligence, accident, or any other cause.

ISBN 978-93-48048-21-9

Cover, Editing, Proofreading & Design : Saarad Majkur, Pune

Printed in India by Sakal Media Pvt. Ltd.

Index

Food Trails Of India : Recipes

Preface

India, with its diverse culture and rich culinary heritage, offers a paradise for food enthusiasts. From aromatic spices to tantalizing street food, the country is a treasure trove of flavours waiting to be explored Traveling in India is all about the discovery of varieties in the Indian culture along with their exotic cuisines.

Indian food is dear to the world because of its rich history, the varied mixture and the warm hospitality with which Indians serve the plates. Indian cuisine is renowned worldwide for its vibrant flavours, colours, tastes, aromatic spices, and diverse culinary traditions.

Indian cuisine is a harmonious blend of diverse regional flavours, cooking techniques, and culinary traditions. From aromatic curries to delicate biryanis, each dish tells a story and offers a unique experience that tantalizes the taste buds.

Street food in India, which has become popular worldwide, is an accessible and affordable way to experience the incredible diversity of Indian flavours.

In this book, I have tried to take readers through some of the most adventurous food trails in India, where they can savour mouth-watering delicacies and experience the vibrant local food culture. I have tried to introduce the food variety available regionally including some typical dishes and recipes. This book has many regional names and phrases that one can hear about while going on such food trails in India. Most of them are explained in simple English language. Hoping the readers will enjoy strolling on this food trail of India hand in hand with me through my writing in this book.

I also take this opportunity to thank Amruta, Jyoti, Ashwini and everyone who helped me through this journey. and most importantly, Sakal Publication for publishing the book.

Indian Food Culture

India is a diverse country with many regional cultures. The food culture of every region is shaped by climate, land and access to natural resources. Each state of India has its own food speciality, different methods of cooking and its unique cuisine that reflects it's culture and tradition. With all the sumptuous dishes, intricate ingredients and tongue-tickling flavours, Indian Cuisine is one of the most popular cuisines in the world.

Indian food is different from the rest of the world; not only in taste but also in cooking methods. One of the important aspects of Indian food is that it is complete and nutritious. The dependence on foreign foods is not required as our legumes, beans, grains, fruits and vegetables provide us with ample amounts of fiber, fat, carbohydrates, proteins, vitamins and minerals. Dairy products like curd, buttermilk and cream are also popular and used by most of the people of India.

Indian food system emphasizes eating agricultural and natural produce "in season, " such as mangoes and sour fruits in summer, leafy vegetables and green beans in monsoon and root vegetables in winter. This is based upon a belief that "in-season" foods are more potent, tastier, and of greater nutritional value. However, the year-round availability of many foods due to technology is beginning to change eating habits.

Food plays an important part in Indian culture. The variety of food showcases Indian cultural diversity. In Indian culture, cooking is considered an art. Preparing a meal from scratch is a centuries-old culinary tradition. Women used to spend a considerable amount of time preparing each Indian delicacy, and this is a custom still observed in many households across the country. Indian people are fond of traditional home made food. Indian meal consists of various flat-breads like Chapati or roti, rice, dals, dry vegetables, curries, chutneys and pickles. Masalas are used in making vegetable and meat dishes as well as condiments like papads, pickles and chutneys are made at home. It is fondly said that in India every kitchen has its own cook book.

Every Indian family has knowledge of cooking acquired through generations. Old women in the family have invented many unique recipes by experimenting and handing them down to new generations. Mothers usually begin to give cooking lessons to their daughters fairly at a young age, passing down family recipes. Indians grow up eating home made food and associate it with warm feelings and good memories. It ties them to their families, holding a special and personal value.

In India, it is firmly believed that 'Family that eats together stays together'. In many families sitting down with their family for a meal is one of the most important activities of the day as it is believed that meal time is a strong source of family bonding, talking and sharing. A traditional Indian kitchen or "rasoi", is a place that originates the warmth and love of Indian cooking.

Indian food culture is one of the oldest and richest food cultures in the world. It is a culinary delight that offers a rich and diverse range offlavours, aromas, and textures. From spicy curries to savoury snacks, Indian cuisine has something to offer for everyone and that is the real beauty of Indian food culture.

Indian Cooking Techniques

Basic Ingredients

To cook Indian food, a kitchen must be stocked with these basic ingredients.

1. Oil, mustard seeds, turmeric powder, asafoetida
2. Coriander and cumin powder
3. Garam masala - A mixture of dry ground spices
4. For wet masala - Garlic, ginger, onions and chillies
5. Any two types of dals like toor dal or moong dal
6. Rice
7. For Chapati - Wheat flour
8. For Curries - Tomato, potato and fresh vegetables

Process of Cooking Indian Food Step by Step

1. Begin with choosing a proper pan and a spoon.
2. Heat oil in a pan and splutter Mustard seeds. Add asafoetida and turmeric powder and sauté.
3. The next step is to shallow fry or sauté wet masala.
4. Add meat or vegetables and continue sautéing.

5. Finally, cook it either by simmering or boiling.

Most of the Indian recipes involve the following three cooking methods.

1. Tempering 2. Sautéing 3. Simmering

However several other cooking techniques give an authentic Indian touch and taste to the food. The following points explain above mentioned cooking methods and such techniques along with some recipes.

Cooking Techniques and Methods to Make Authentic Indian Food

There are different methods used to cook food like frying, boiling, sautéing, steaming and grilling. Indian cooking involves all the above methods plus a few more special techniques. Many Indian dishes use a combination of three to four kinds of cooking methods.

Tempering and Tadka are the most important steps used in Indian cooking.

1. Tempering

The first step in making any Indian dish is the tempering of spices. It is a traditional method to extract the full flavour from spices. Basic ingredients used in tempering are mustard seeds, cumin seeds, asafoetida and turmeric powder.

How to make tempering

Heat oil/ghee in a pan. When the oil is hot enough lower the flame and add mustard seeds/cumin seeds. When they start crackling add asafoetida and turmeric powder. Once the tempering is complete add vegetables, dal or meat and cook.

2. Tadka

Tadka is a tempering commonly used as the finishing touch to a dish. Hot tadka is poured on the food at the end of cooking or just before serving.

Usually, tadka is made with ghee using cumin seeds, curry leaves, garlic, red chillies, and spices. The combination of spices used depends on the dish being prepared as well as the region in which it is being prepared. In short, tadka is famous all across India but the methods vary perregion.

When spices are added to oil, they release their aromas and flavours, which the oil captures and carries into the food or dish prepared. It enhances the flavour and taste of the dish.

Tadka is used for chutney, dhokla, curd rice, curries, dal and many such dishes.

How to make tadka :
In a tadka pan heat 2 tea spoons of oil. When it's hot, add ¼ tsp mustard seeds, 3 to 4 curry leaves and 1 broken red chilli. When they start crackling add a pinch of asafoetida. Pour hot tadka onto the prepared dish.

Depending on the dish prepared, the ingredients to make tadka may vary. Some recipes might need cumin seeds instead of mustard seeds, and garlic cloves instead of curry leaves. Thus, at times, such varied items can be used while making tadka.

Some examples of dishes that use the Tadka technique are as follows :

Lasooni Dal Tadka

Lasooni Dal Tadka is a popular Indian dish, where cooked dal is finished with tadka made with ghee and spices. The main flavour in this Dal is garlic.

Ingredients :

For Dal : 1 cup cooked dal - Mixture of Tur dal and Masoor dal, 1 tomato, 10 flacks of garlic, 1 tsp of garam masala, 1 table spoon of chopped coriander leaves. 1 tsp oil, and salt to taste.

For tadka : 1 tbsp ghee, ¼ tsp cumin seeds, 3-4 flakes of garlic, 1 red chilli, a pinch of asafoetida, turmeric powder.

Method : Chop tomato and garlic. Mash Dal with water. In a pan heat oil and fry chopped garlic and tomato. Sauté for some time. Add a little water and cook. When tomato and garlic are cooked, add dal mixture, garam masala and salt. Bring to a boil. Top with chopped coriander. Make tadka and pour it on the dal.

Dahi Tadka

Ingredients : 2 cups thick yoghurt, 1 tbsp milk, 1 tsp each, mustard seeds, and cumin seeds, a pinch of asafoetida, sugar and salt to taste, 1 dried red chilli, 1 tbsp chopped coriander leaves and 1 tsp ghee or oil.

Method : Mix curd with milk. Add salt, sugar and coriander leaves to the curd. Heat ghee in a tadka pan . Add mustard seeds and cumin seeds. When they crackle lower the heat and add asafoetida and red chilli. Let it cool for some time. Pour this tadka on curd and mix well.

Curd Raita laced with a tadka of cumin seeds and mustard seeds pairs perfectly with pulao, biryani or Roti. We can make different types of raitas by adding Boondi or chopped cucumber or onion to dahi tadka.

3. Bhuna

The word Bhuna means 'to fry' and refers to the cooking style. In other words, the Indian version of sautéing is called *bhuna*. A *bhuna* tends to be made with meat or vegetables that are cooked in their own juices resulting in a gravy that has deep richness and flavour. This method involves cooking on a low flame with the addition of a little water from time to time to prevent the spices or the food from burning.

Some examples of dishes that use the Bhuna technique or style are as follows :

Bhuna Gosht

Ingredients : 500 grams of boneless mutton, 3 chopped onions, 2 chopped tomatoes, 1 tsp garlic paste, 1 tbsp thick curd, 1 tsp ginger paste, 2 tsp cumin powder, 3 tsp coriander powder, 1 tsp red chilli powder, 1 tsp garam masala, 5 tbsps oil, a pinch of turmeric powder and salt to taste. Coriander leaves for garnishing.

Method : Mix curd, ginger paste, garlic paste turmeric powder and salt. Apply it to the mutton. Keep aside for an hour. Heat 1 oil in a pan and fry the mutton. In another thick-bottomed pan add remaining oil and fry onion till golden brown. Add tomatoes and fry for a few minutes. Add mutton, cumin powder, coriander powder garam masala, and chilli powder and mix well. Continue frying. Cover and Sprinklea little water if required. Keep stirring till the mutton is cooked. Typically, Bhuna Gosht is cooked slowly over medium heat for around 45 minutes to one hour, allowing the meat to become tender. We need to be patient when cooking Bhuna gosht.

4. DumPukth

Dum Pukth means cooking food in its own steam. The food is cooked in an enclosed container, where the steam is not allowed to escape. Dum is an excellent way of cooking which keeps the flavours and nutrients intact.

Dum means 'to breathe slowly' and Pukht means 'process of cooking', thus Dum Pukht means 'cooking slowly on slow fire'. In this method, the food is cooked in a sealed pot over long periods. Slow cooking infuses the flavours from the various spices, herbs, and fats and imparts various aromas and certain, unique juiciness to the food.

Dum cooking is commonly associated with Mughlai cuisine and has its roots in Persian or Central Asian cooking.

5. Tandoor

Tandoor is the most traditional and popular cooking method used in India. A tandoor is a cylindrical clay oven in which food is cooked over charcoal. It is used to make unleavened flatbreads like nan and roti and to roast different meats,

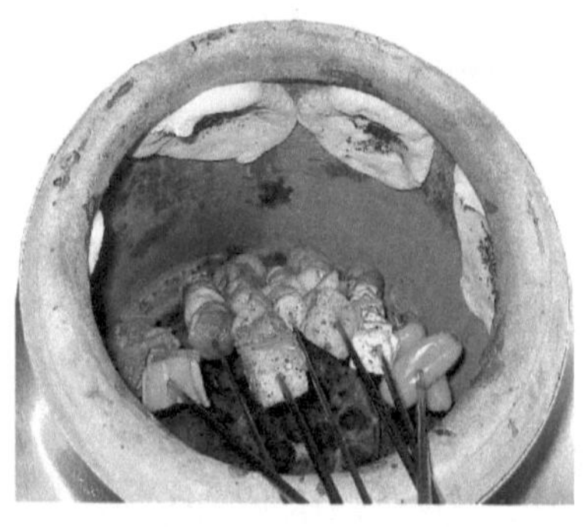

The food cooked in a tandoor oven is called Tandoori.

Some of the famous tandoor dishes are tandoori chicken, fish tikka, paneer tikka, tandoori roti and naan. Marination is an important part of tandoori cooking. Almost all tandoori dishes have yoghurt as their base. Many herbs and spices are used to give exclusive flavour to dishes. The meats are coloured a bright orange-red witha natural tandoor colour added to the marinade. The marinated meat is threaded on long skewers and placed vertically in the oven. Naan and Rotis are pressed against the inner side of the oven.

Tandoor Marinade

Ingredients : 2 cups plain yoghurt, 2 tbsps garlic paste, 1 tbsp ginger paste, 1 tbsp each cumin powder and coriander powder, ½ tbsp black pepper, pinch of turmeric powder, 1 tsp salt and red food colour.

Method : Mix the ginger paste and garlic paste with yoghurt. Add cumin powder, coriander powder, pepper, salt and food colour and mix well. This marinade helps to tenderise, spice up and flavourise the meat or vegetables.

Tandoor chicken

Ingredients : 6 chicken thighs, juice of 1 lemon, tandoor marinade.

Method : Using a sharp knife, make slits on chicken thighs. Squeeze lemon juice all over the chicken thighs. Cover the chicken pieces with the marinade and keep aside for eight

to ten hours. Thread it on the skewer and cook it in the tandoor oven.

Serve hot with mint chutney and onion.

Paneer Tikka

Ingredients : 250 grams paneer, 1 large capsicum, 1 tomato and 1 onion, tandoor marinade.

Method : Make 1. 5-inch squares of paneer, cut capsicum and onion intoa square shape, and Slice tomato. Apply tandoor marinadeon paneer and vegetables and keep aside for eight

hours, Thread paneer piece, tomato slice, onion and capsicum on the skewer and cook in the tandoor oven.

Serve hot with mint chutney.

6. Dhungar

Dhungar is an ancient technique of smoking and infusing the flavour of burnt charcoal smoke into food. Dhungar means to impart a smoky flavour to the food. The key ingredient in dhungar is ghee, a clarified butter. A small cup with red-hot charcoal is kept atop the food in the main pot and a spoonful of ghee is drizzled on the charcoal. Then the pot is sealed with a tight-fitting lid or foil. Thus, trapping the smoke and allowing it to infuse and perfume the food. Just before eating, the cup of charcoal is removed.

The dhungar method is a South Asian way of introducing buttery and smoky flavour as a finishing touch to food. It involves a reaction between ghee and hot coals in a lidded pot that produces a smoky and buttery aroma which can perfume any food that you put and trap inside such pot.

Indian Spices

Mention Indian cuisine, and people will imagine the spicy-hot food, but this is not the reality. The spices are the magical ingredient of Indian cooking. Indian food is widely appreciated for its use of herbs and spices. They are the heart and soul of Indian cooking. The secret of traditional and delicious Indian food is the flavour of rich spices.

India plays an important role in the spice market of the world. In ancient times majority of the spices were produced in India and exported worldwide. Spices are defined using terms like seed, fruit, root, bark, or such parts of plants. They are used for flavouring, colouring or preserving food. They are used in different forms like whole, chopped, ground, roasted, sautéed and fried. Every single spice used in Indian dishes carries some or the other nutritional as well as medicinal properties.

There are following three categories of Indian spices :

1. Basic Spices
2. Complementary Spices
3. Aromatic Spices

Basic Spices

Basic or primary spices are those which are used in everyday Indian cooking. Basic spices include the following spices :

1. Cumin

Cumin is a dried seed of a plant known as Cuminum cyminum. It is one of the most popular spices and is commonly used in the cuisines of Latin America, the Middle East, North Africa and India. It is available in the form of whole dried seeds or as powder. The most common variety of cumin is of brownish-yellow colour.

2. Coriander seeds

Coriander is a feathery annual plant of the parsley family. All parts of this plant are used as a spice and herb. Aromatic leaves and dried seeds are the most commonly used forms in Indian cuisine. Yellowish brown dry seeds of the plant are called coriander seeds. They are usually roasted and ground before using.

3. Mustard Seeds

Mustard seeds are the small round seeds of the mustard plant. These seeds are about 1 to 2 millimetres in diameter. They come in yellow, white and black colour. Black seeds are stronger in flavour than the yellow or white ones. They can be ground into

a powder or used as a whole. They are often added to hot oil to bring out the flavour.

All parts of the mustard plant are edible, including the seeds, leaves, and flowers. Mustard seeds can be used in many ways in the kitchen. They are added to vegetable or meat dishes to kick up the flavour and heat. Ground mustard seeds can be used to make mustard sauces, salad dressings and marinades. Mix it with water or vinegar to make your own home made mustard.

Mustard oil, which has a distinctive pungent taste, is used in cooking and for medicinal purposes.

4. Turmeric

Turmeric is a strong, golden-orange spice. It comes from the root of a native Asian plant and has been used in cooking for hundreds of years. The roots of turmeric are boiled in water, dried, and then powdered.

Turmeric powder gives its flavour and yellow colour to the food. Turmeric has been used in both Ayurvedic medicine as an anti-inflammatory, to treat digestive and liver problems, skin diseases, and wounds.

Fresh turmeric roots and leaves are also used in Indian cooking.

5. Asafoetida

Asafoetida is a dried gum extracted from the plant ferula's sapling. It has a pungent smell. Dried and powdered asafoetida is used to give flavour to curries, dal and vegetables. It is an effective remedy for several diseases related to the stomach and aids in relieving gaseous problems.

Complimentary Spices

Complimentary spices are the additional spices which enrich and complement the prepared dish along with the basic spices.

1. Fenugreek plant's seeds and leaves feature in Indian cooking as a spice. Fenugreek seeds have a strong fragrance. They are dried and used as a spice. They are commonly called Kasuri methi.

2. Fennel Seeds are used as a culinary herb as well as a medicinal plant. They are sometimes used in tempering butare widely used to prepare curry pastes and spice mixes. They are also used as an after-meal digestive. Fennel seeds are the key ingredient in the candied mouth fresheners that you find in Indian restaurants.

3. Ginger powder is used as a spice which has a nice smell and sharp taste. It is extracted from the dried ginger root. Dry ginger powder is widely used in the kitchen to add flavour and aroma. It Is commonly used in masala, curries and stews. When added to tea, it gives a soothing effect.

4. Cinnamon is the rolled inner bark of a tree having fragrance. There are two main types of cinnamon, Ceylon and Cassia. This spice is used in both sweet and savoury dishes. It has been used medicinally for thousands of years and is known for its health benefits.

5. Cloves are small flower buds of the clove tree. The buds are harvested and then dried. Whole cloves are shaped like a small, reddish-brown spike, usually around 1 centimetre in length, with a bulbous top. Cloves can be used in whole or ground. They have

a very strong flavour and aroma. It is one of the most valuable spices that has been used for centuries in cooking and for many medicinal purposes.

6. Black pepper is a flowering vine cultivated for its fruit called peppercorn. It is usually dried and used as a spice and seasoning. This has been used in Indian kitchens even before chillies entered the country.

7. Black cardamom is larger than green cardamom and is used only in Indian curries. The seeds of black cardamom have a strong aroma so it is used in small quantities.

8. Bay leaves are known for their flavour and fragrance. It isused in cooking, either dried or fresh, and is removed from the dish before consumption, it is not used in ground form.

9. Ajwain also called bishop's weed, is aherb that is used as a spice and a major ingredient in different types of medicines. The seeds of ajwain are

small yet have a sharp pungent aroma. A small amount of ajwain is added as a flavouring agent while preparing the dough for many Indian flat-breads.

10. Mace is the outer covering of nutmeg with a similar aroma. In Indian cuisine, it is often used in Biryanis, curries and meat dishes.

11. Sesame Seeds are tiny oil-rich seeds. They are rich in calcium. Both white and black sesame seeds are widely used in Indian cuisine. Black sesame seeds are unhulled, and the white ones are hulled with the skins removed.

12. Black stone flower is one of the less known Indian spices, but a popular one among the regions in the western coastline and southern India. It is popularly known as dagad phool in Marathi, one of the local languages

of the state of Maharashtra. It is used for making a traditional Maharashtrian spice mix called goda masala.

Aromatic Spices
Aromatic spices are spices that have a pleasant smell.

1. Saffron
This is the most expensive spice in the world. The best saffron is dark orange and comes from Kashmir, Iran

or Spain. Fresh saffron has a deep colour and unique flavour.

Saffron is used in small quantities. It is usually dissolved in warm water or milk before being added to dishes.

2. Green cardamom

This aromatic spice is widely used in Indian cuisine. They are used whole or in powder form in both sweet and savoury Indian dishes. From biryani to chai, Indians love it in everything for its beautiful sweet smell and flavour.

3. Nutmeg

Nutmeg is a seed of the Myristica fragrans tree. It is an incredibly intense spice with a strong and distinctive aroma. It is used in powder form in sweet and savoury dishes. It is commonly used in Indian sweets.

Interesting Facts About Spices

- Cardamom is called The Queen of Spices.
- Pepper is called the king of spice.
- In the ancient world, pepper was so valuable that it was used as currency to trade.
- Saffron and cardamom are called the royal spices of Indian sweets.
- Cinnamon is one of the oldest spices known to a man.
- Turmeric is called superfood spice. It ranks very high on the list of the world's healthiest spices.

Indian Herbs

India has been the land of herbs, spices and Ayurvedic medicines since ancient ages. Herbs and spices were being used for their medicinal value before they found their way into our kitchens.

Herbs are the leafy part of a plant that is used in cooking for seasoning and flavouring. Herbs can be used fresh or dried. Fresh herbs are generally delicately flavoured, so are added to the dishat the end. They add flavour and colour to the food or drink butin addition to that they have their own set of health-promoting properties.

Most of the herbs are high in aroma and full of flavour. They are truly a chef's delight in preparing meals to please all kinds of palates. They boost the flavour, looks and texture of the meal.

Here are a few Indian Herbs which are used in cooking and Ayurvedic medicines.

1. Garlic (Lasun)

Garlic is found in the form of a bulb. It is covered in inedible skin and comprises many cloves. Beneath the skin, there is a fleshy bulb which is used for cooking. Garlic is powerful and pungent, yet aromatic when cooked.

Garlic   Ginger   Mint

Coriander   Curry leaves   Dill

Garlic cloves are used raw while cooking and have a strong flavour and aroma which bring simple food to life. In most of the dishes garlic is sautéed with onions, fried in tadka or to make garlic bread or salad dressing.

2. Ginger (Adrak)

Ginger is a root of the plant with a slightly biting taste. It is used driedas well as fresh. Dry ginger powder is called Sunth, in Marathi and is used in tea masala or Kashmiri cuisine. Ground ginger is used to flavour breads, sauces, curry dishes or pickles.

3. Mint (Pudina)

This refreshing herb has found its way into the Indian kitchen in multiple ways. You can find fresh mint in chutneys, raita or yoghurt relish and salads. It is also used in parathas, kababs and biryanis. There are different variations of mint pulao or mint rice across India.

Mint leaves create a cool sensation in the mouth. Thus, toothpaste, mouthwash, breath mints, and chewing gums are flavoured with mint.

4. Coriander or Cilantro.

Coriander leaves is heavily used in Indian cuisine, especially as a garnish. Adding fresh coriander leaves as a garnish toward the end enhances the flavour and appearance of the dish. They are used in assorted chutneys, and the most popular one is green chutney.

5. Curry leaves

Curry leaves are one of the popular herbs in India. They are also known as sweet neem, as they look like neem leaves but are not bitter. Adding a handful of curry leaves during tempering adds a distinct flavour to curries and gravies. We can also make chutneys and spice powders with dried curry leaves. The fresh leaves are an indispensable part of Indian cuisine and traditional medicines. They are most widely used in South Indian cuisine.

6. Dill

Dill has a different but beautiful fragrance and taste. It can be used to make a vegetable, mixed with dough to make flatbreads and added to Dal or curries for extra flavour.

7. Green chillies

Green chillies are the life and soul of Indian meals. Without a touch of a chilli, dish is incomplete. Slit, sliced, chopped or diced, chilis are added to the food to give a spicy and tangy flavour. They are grown through out the year and available in fresh, powdered or pickled. Deep-fried chilis are a popular accompaniment in Indian street food like Vada pav, Samosa or Bhaji.

Masalas & Gravies

Different types of *masalas are* used in Indian cooking in different ways.

Masala is a mixture of ground spices used in Indian cooking. It is a combination of dried spices or a spice paste. The following are different ways in which masalas are used while cooking.

1. Khada Masala : Khada means whole spices. The spices like cinnamon, cloves, green cardamom, black cardamom, and cumin are tempered into hot oil while cooking to allow the flavours to infuse with the oil.

2. Potli Masala : Potli means a sachet or a pouch of spices. Spices are tied up in a muslin bag and left in a curry or liquid to let the flavours be infused. There can be many variations of the potli masala.

Potli is added for easy removal of the spices after they have infused their flavours and aroma with the liquid. It is used to flavour curries and also to flavour the water or stock for biryani.

3. Wet Masala : Wet masalas are made by soaking the spices in liquid and grinding them into a fine paste. Fresh ingredients like ginger, garlic, coriander leaves, and green chillies are used in wet masalas.

4. Dry or Powdered Masala : There are hundreds of different masalas in Indian cooking. They are prepared for a particular dish, for example, *Pav Bhaji masala* for *Pav Bhaji, Sambar masala* for *sambar* or *Biryani masala* for *biryani* etc.

A few of the famous dry masalas in Indian cooking are Garam Masala, Chole Masala, Chaat Masala, Tandoori Masala, Chicken Masala, and Chai Masala.

The following are a few famous and special masalas used by Indians in different regions.

- **Pach Phoran**

It is a Bengali spice mix. It is a blend of five spices namely cumin seeds, fennel seeds, fenugreek seeds, mustard seeds and nigella seeds. Bengali cuisine is incomplete without nigella seeds. Its medicinal properties make it an important part of dal and curries.

Garam Masala

Garam masala is a blend of eight or more spices and each family has their own secret recipe. However, the general recipe for the garam masala is as follows :

Ingredients : 2 tbsp coriander seeds, 1 tbsp cumin seeds, 10 cloves, 15 peppercorns, ½ tsp cardamom seeds, 2 inch cinnamon, 3 bay leaves, ¼ tsp nutmeg powder, 5 dry red chillies- optional

Method : Roast the spices separately using a little oil. Cool and grind to a smooth powder.

Goda or Kala Masala

Goda masala is a special spice blend of Maharashtra. In the Marathi language, goda means sweet. However, goda masala is not sweet by taste but its aroma is sweet. Also due to its black colour, few people call it Kala Masala.

The following is the recipe for Goda Masala.

Ingredients : 3 cups coriander Seeds, 1 cup cumin seeds, 4" cinnamon sticks, 15 black peppercorns, 10 cloves, 4 bay leaves, 5 dagadphool/ stone flowers. 1 cup desiccated coconut, 1/2 cup sesame seeds, 1/2 tsp asafoetida powder, 1 tsp turmeric powder, 2 tsp chilli powder and salt to taste. 4 tsp oil.

Method : In a large pan put some oil and roast coriander seeds and cummin seeds separately. In remaining oil roast peppercorns, bay leaves, cinnamon, cloves and dagad fool. Roast these ingredients till aromatic. Keep aside to cool. Dry roast desiccated coconut and sesame seeds. Grind coriander seeds, cummin seeds and other roasted masalas to make a fine powder. Grind coconut and sesame seeds and add to the powdered masala. Lastly add asafoetida powder, turmeric powder, chilli powder and salt. Mix well and store it in an airtight container.

Different Types of Gravies in Indian Cooking

Gravy is the soul of Indian cuisine. It is a thick liquid that gives body and flavour to the curries and other food preparations. It has a saucy consistency. For the base of delicious Indian curries, different types of gravies are used.

1. White Gravy

Ingredients : 4 onions, 20 cashew nuts, 1 tbsp ginger garlic paste, a pinch of cardamom powder, 2 bay leaves, 2 green chillies, 1 cup yoghurt, 1 tbsp oil and salt to taste.

Method : Chop onions and boil them in water for 10 minutes. Drain and grind to smooth paste. Soak cashew nuts in warm water for 15–20 minutes and then grind to a smooth paste.

Heat oil in a non-stick pan and add onion paste, ginger garlic paste, cardamom powder, bay leaves and green chillies. Sauté and add cashew paste. Mix well by adding some water. Cook on low flame till oil separates. Whisk yoghurt and add to this mixture. Add salt and cook for 5 minutes.

2. Yellow gravy

Yellow gravy is prepared by adding turmeric to the white gravy.

3. Red Gravy

Ingredients : 4 onions, 5 tomatoes, ginger paste and garlic paste, 2 tsps each, 1 tbsp turmeric powder, 1 tsp chilli powder, 3 tbsp oil and salt.

Method : Put tomatoes in boiling water. Cover and keep aside, when cool take out the skin and mash. Chop onions. Heat 1 tbsp oil in a non-stick pan and sauté chopped onion. Add ginger garlic paste and tomatoes. Cook for 5 minutes. Add turmeric powder, red chilli powder, salt and mix well. Cool and grind to a smooth paste. In the same pan heat the remaining 2 tbsp oil and sauté this paste till oil separates.

There are many methods to make red gravy. A quicker method is to make it in a pressure cooker or by using tomato paste or tomato puree instead of fresh ones.

4. Brown Gravy

The method for making brown gravy is the same as red gravy. Just add 1 tbsp garam masala, 1 tbsp coriander powder and ½ tbsp cumin powder and sauté.

5. Shahi Gravy

Ingredients : 3 onions, 15 cashew nuts, 10 almonds, 1 tbsp poppy seeds, 1 tbsp ginger garlic paste, 1 bay leaf, salt, 2 tbsp ghee, 1 tbsp grated khoya, 2 tbsp fresh cream.

Method : Chop onions and boil them in water for 10 minutes. Drain and grind to smooth paste. Soak cashew nuts and almonds in warm water for 15 – 20 minutes. Skin the almonds. Roast poppy seeds. Grind cashew nuts, almonds and poppy seeds to smooth paste. Heat the ghee in a non-stick pan and sauté onion paste. Add bay leaf and ground paste and sauté till ghee separates. Add grated khoya and cook for some time. Lastly, add salt.

Indian dishes made with shahi gravy are always garnished with fresh cream. **Saffron** is also added to shahi gravy for colour, flavour and aroma.

Khoya is a dairy product which is widely used in Indian gravies. To make khoya whole milk is thickened by heating in an open iron pan.

6. Green Gravy

Ingredients : 1 cup freshly grated coconut, 1 cup finely cut coriander leaves, 4 green chillies, salt and ½ cup fresh mint leaves – optional
Method : Put all the ingredients in a blender. Add water and blend to make a smooth paste.

7. Green Gravy with Spinach

Ingredients : 3 cups spinach leaves, 1 tsp ginger paste, 1 tsp garlic paste, 2 onions finely chopped, 4 green chillies, 1 cup coriander leaves, 2 tbsp oil, salt.
Method : Put spinach leaves in water and boil. Cover and keep for 2-3 minutes. Take out spinach leaves and put them in iced water. Drain them.

Heat oil in a pan and sauté chopped onion. Add ginger paste, garlic paste, green chillies, coriander leaves and salt and sauté. Turn off the flame and add spinach. Put all ingredients in a blender with some water and make a smooth paste.

Curries

India is called the land of curries. There are numerous types of curries in India. Curry dishes are usually thick and spicy and are eaten with rice and a variety of Indian breads. Indian curries are as diverse as India. Like types of oils, spices and ingredients each state in India has a different kind of curry. These curries are mostly made of vegetables, meat, chicken or fish.

Each curry has its unique character, body, flavour, and texture. Here are some of the curries from different Indian states.

Bengal : Bengali curries are made in mustard oil using their unique blend of five spices- which is called pachphoran.

Kerala : Different kinds of fish curries and *gassi* are famous Kerala curries. In Kerala, coconut milk and tamarind pulp are used in fish curry. Fresh grated coconut and onion are used in Prawn gassi. Most of the vegetable and meat curries are cooked in coconut oil using fresh coconut, curry leaves and lots of spices.

Goa : Goan curries like *Sorpotel* and *vindaloo* are vinegar-based pork curries.

Kashmir : Curries like *rogan josh* are made in pure ghee using brown onion, kashmiri chillies and saffron along with other spices.

Punjab : Famous punjabi curries like *butter chicken* and *kofta curry* are made with tomato and onion puree, spices and a lot of fresh cream.

Rajasthan : Vegetarian curries like *gatteki sabji* and *kadhi pakore* are made using pure ghee, gram flour and yoghurt.

South India : Curries like *rasam, sambar* are made using pulses and tamarind pulp.

Maharashtra curries are made in ground nut oil using kala or *goda masala* and little jaggery. Kala/Goda masala is an essential maharashtrian spice powder which is used in everyday cooking to make maharashtrian-style curries, dals and vegetables.

The fusion of exotic spices and different base ingredients like yoghurt, gram flour, onion paste and coconut is the key to creating aromatic and flavourful curries. A little bit of sweet, a little bit of sour, a little bit of spicy and hot taste gives Indian curries a special charm.

Egg Curry

Egg curry or Anda curry is a very common curry dish in most parts of India. There are many ways of making egg curry. It is very easy to prepare. Eggs are first boiled, peeled, and then simmered in the onion tomato-based gravy.

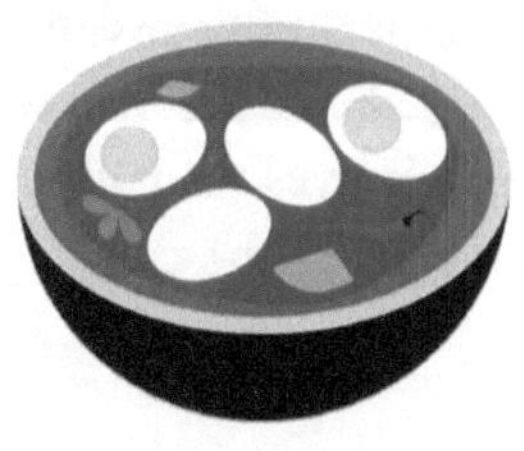

Ingredients : 4 hard-boiled eggs, 2 onions finely chopped, ½ cup Tomato puree, 1 tbsp of ginger garlic paste, 1 tsp of cumin seed, a pinch of turmeric powder, 2 tsps coriander powder, 1 tsp garam masala, 3 tbsp oil, chopped coriander, salt and chilli powder as per taste.

Method : Heat oil in a pan and add cumin seeds. When they start to splutter add chopped onion and sauté for two minutes.

Add turmeric powder, ginger garlic paste and tomato puree. Cook for a minute. Add coriander powder, garam masala, chilli powder and salt. Mix well. Add some water and cook. Lastly, add boiled eggs and chopped coriander. Simmer. Cut eggs into half length-wise and serve with curry.

Kadhi

Ingredients : 2 cups yoghurt, 1/2 cup gram flour, 5 curry leaves, 1/2 tsp pure ghee, 1 tsp cumin seeds, 1-inch ginger, 2 green chillies, sugar and salt to taste. Chopped coriander leaves.

Method : Put curd, gram flour, ginger, salt, sugar and one cup of water into a mixer bowl. Mix well. Heat pure ghee in a pan and add cumin seeds. When they start to splutter add Green chillis and curry leaves. Add curd mixture and let it boil over medium flame. Stir it and add some water if required. Simmer for a few minutes. Add coriander and serve hot with Khichadi or rice.

This dish has many variations based on region and spices. A Punjabi Kadhi is made with Besan (gram flour) Pakoras, Gujarati Kadhi is on the sweeter side, Marwari kadhi is made with spices and red chillies where as Maharashtrian kadhi is made with curry leaves and little jaggery. In some states vegetables like spinach, methi, potato or lady's fingers are added to kadhi.

Rice

Rice is a vital ingredient in all the different cuisines of India. Apart from plain steamed rice, a variety of rice dishes are made in indian cuisine. Rice is consumed at least once a day by most people in one form or the other. In south indian cuisine, rice is eaten for all three meals of the day.

To prepare perfect rice it is important to take the right amount of water and rice. In other words, water to rice ratio is very important. Before making rice rinse it under cold water until the water runs clear and then let it soak for a few minutes. This helps get rid of starch which makes the grains stick together. Drain the rice and then cook it.

Here are some of the popular indian rice dishes.

- **Jeera rice** is a popular north indian dish. Rice is made in pure ghee and flavoured with lots of cumin seeds.
- **Khichadi** is a simple, healthy and tasty dish made with rice, moong dal and spices.
- **Curd rice** is the ultimate comfort food. It is a very common dish in southern indian states and maharashtra. Cooked rice is mixed with curd, and salt and finished with tempering of green chilli, curry leaves and mustard seeds. It is garnished with chopped coriander, pomegranate, shredded carrot or

cucumber. Curd rice is served at the end of a meal to balance the spicy food.

- **Pulao** is one of the most famous Indian rice dishes. Pulao is made by sautéing washed rice in ghee along with various spices, cashew nuts, and raisins and then cooked in vegetable stock. There are many kinds of pulao recipes made in India. Pea's pulao, tawa pulao, vegetable pulao, paneer pulao, kofta pulao and meat pulao are some of the tasty pulao.
- **Chitranna** is a widely prepared rice dish in southern India. Cooked rice is cooled and seasoned with mustard seeds, turmeric powder fried lentils, peanuts, curry leaves, chilli and lemon juice or raw mango.
- **Rice Kheer** is a famous Indian sweet which is easy to make with basic ingredients like rice, milk sugar and nuts. The taste and ingredients used for making phirni and kheer are almost the same. But the difference is in texture, cooking method and serving method.
- **Phirni** is a traditional north indian rice pudding made with rice, milk, sugar and nuts. Slow cooking is the key to making a perfect phirni. The ground rice granules are slow-cooked in milk to a creamy and thick consistency.

  Phirni is served in small earthen bowls called matka. These earthen bowls absorb the extra moisture and liquids and make it thicker. They also infuse the rice pudding with an earthy aroma.
- **South Indian Rice** cuisine is deeply intertwined with rice, which is a staple food in that region. Rice holds significant culinary importance and it is consumed in various forms and preparations throughout the day.

  Tamarind Rice, sesame rice, lemon rice, coconut rice, and bisibelli are some of the famous rice dishes of south india.

Biryani

Biryani, a flavourful rice dish of Persian origin has become a popular celebratory dish in India. There are many stories about how biryani made its way to India, but it has since spread  to all parts of the country with numerous local and regional variations.

Biryani is a layered rice preparation, traditionally made with spiced meat. This royal Indian dish is a complete meal itself. While making biryani long-grained Basmati rice is cooked with spices like cardamom, cinnamon and saffron. Cooked rice and cooked meat are added in alternate layers and the whole pot is steamed over a low flame with a sealed lid on top of it.

The main components of biryani are basmati rice, meat, marinade, onion, herbs and spices. The meat is usually marinated in fried onions, spices and yoghurt as it helps to tenderize the meat. Biryani is often topped with dry fruits, saffron and herbs like fresh mint and coriander leaves.

There are countless versions of biryani, made by substituting and altering ingredients, spices and cooking methods. The following are a few of the famous indian biryanis.

- **Hyderabadi Biryani :** This is one of the most popular types of biryanis in India. It is made of goat meat that is marinated and cooked along with the rice and is seasoned with coconut and saffron.
- **Lucknowi Biryani :** This type of biryani is based on a Persian cooking style so it uses the dumpukht method where the meat and gravy are only cooked partially and are then layered and served in a sealed handi.
- **Mughlai Biryani :** This biryani is cooked with curd, chicken, almond paste, ghee, dry fruits, and green chillies, and has a rich flavour.

Though there are endless types of biryanis; they are cooked with three main methods. Each of these methods gives a different taste to the biryani.

1. **Dum Biryani :** Parboiled rice and raw marinated meat are placed into a thick-bottomed pot. The pot is sealed with dough and cooked on dum for hours.
2. **Pukki Biryani :** Rice and meat are cooked separately. They are layered in a pot and steamed.
3. **Kacchi Biryani :** Raw marinated meat is put at the bottom of the pot and topped with half-cooked rice. The pot is sealed and biryani is cooked on a slow flame.

Basmati Rice

Long-grain basmati rice is a speciality of India. It is considered one of the best-quality white rice. When cooked, each grain remains separate and leaves a nice aroma. It is used to make dishes like biryani and pulao. The name Basmati is derived from the Hindi word 'Baas' which means fragrance.

Basmati rice hails from the foothills of the himalayas in northern India. The slender grains of basmati rice elongate at least twice their original size with a soft and fluffy texture upon cooking. With delicious taste, superior aroma and distinct flavour, basmati rice is unique among other aromatic long-grain rice varieties.

Indian traders introduced basmati rice to the middle east through cultural exchange and since then it has become an important part of middle eastern cuisines. Today basmati rice is one of the most widely used ingredients of many cuisines across the globe. Its unique taste and aroma are the main reason for its worldwide popularity and success.

The following are a few famous recipes made using long-grain Basmati rice.

Kashmiri Saffron Pulao

Ingredients : 1 cup basmati rice, 1 tbsp ghee, 1/4 tsp saffron, ½ cup milk, 1 cup mixed dry fruits, 2 cardamoms, 1 bay leaf, 2 cinnamon sticks, 6 cloves, 2 cups water and salt to taste.

Method : Soak saffron in luck warm milk for 10 minutes. Wash and soak basmati rice in water for 30 minutes. Heat the ghee in a pan and sauté dry fruits. When golden brown, remove from ghee and keep aside. Add cardamom, bay leaf, cinnamon and cloves tothe pan and stir. Add drained rice and sauté for 2-3 minutes. Add 2 cups water and salt. Cover and let the rice cook on law flame. When rice is half cooked mix the saffron milk with rice. Cover and cook for 5 minutes. Remove rice from the flame and mix dry fruits into the rice. Serve hot with curry.

Tomato Rice

Ingredients : 1 tbsp oil, 1 onion chopped, 1 cup tomato puree, 1 ½ cup long grain rice, 3 cup vegetable stock, ½ cup cashew nuts, 1 tbsp ginger garlic paste, 1 tsp cumin seeds and ½ cup chopped coriander. Salt to taste.

Method : Soak rice for 10 minutes and drain. Chop onion. Heat oil in a pressure cooker and splutter cumin seeds. Add rice, chopped onion, ginger garlic paste, salt and cashew nuts. Sauté well and add tomato puree and vegetable stock. Mix well. Pressure Cook for 2 whistles. Let the steam escape before opening the lid. Garnish with chopped coriander and serve.

Mutter or Green Peas Rice (Matar Bhat)

Ingredients : 1 cup rice, 3/4 cup green peas, 2/3 curry leaves, 1" piece cinnamon, 3 cloves, pinch of asafoetida, ½ tsp turmeric powder, ½ tsp mustard seeds, 1 tsp cumin powder, 1 tbsp goda masala, 1 tbsp oil, salt and sugar to taste, few cashew nuts, 3 cups of water, 1 tbsp fresh coconut, 1 tbsp fresh coriander

Method : Soak rice for 10 minutes and drain. Heat oil in a pressure cooker and splutter mustard seeds. Add asafoetida, turmeric powder, cinnamon, cloves, cashew nuts and peas. Sauté well and add rice, cumin powder, goda masala and water. Mix well. Pressure cook for 2 whistles. Let the steam escape before opening the lid. Garnish with coriander and fresh coconut.

>>>>>>

Naan, Chapati & Roti

When we think about indian cuisine, the first thing that comes to mind is the different kinds of flatbreads. Flat*breads are an integral part of Indian cuisine and served with numerous tasty dishes and curries. There is a huge variety of Indian breads, ranging from flatbreads to crepes, using leavened and unleavened dough.

Different regions of India have their own ingredients and styles of baking bread. Whether puffy, layered, fried or tandoor baked, breads play an important part in Indian cuisine. There are more than thirty types of breads in India which are consumed at breakfast, tea time or as a part of the main meal. Their variation reflects the diversity of Indian culture and food habits.

Punjab is known as the "bread basket of India, " The bread basket of the country is an are a which, because of the richness of the soil and advantageous climate, produces large quantities of wheat and other grain. Punjab is a land of rivers and it has the most fertile soil which is ideal for the production of wheat. Naturally different types of breads made with wheat flour are part of the daily meals of people living here.

The Popular Breads of India.

1. Naan

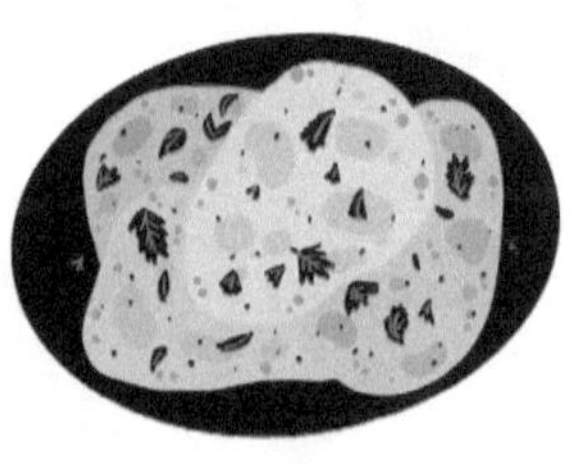

A flatbread prepared with all-purpose flour, wheat flour or a combination of both is the most famous Indian bread. This fluffy, leavened indian flatbread is best served hot, with curry, vegetables or meat dishes. Naan is traditionally cooked in a clay tandoor oven. Apart from plain naan, kheema stuffed naan and garlic or mint-flavoured naan are also very popular.

2. Chapati

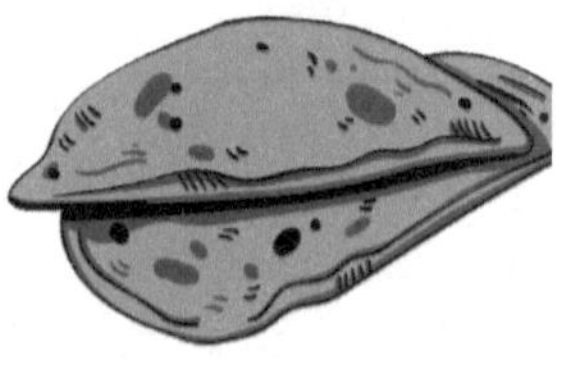

Chapati is one of the most common Indian breads. This unleavened flatbread is made from whole wheat flour. A pinch of salt and a little oil is added while kneading the dough with water. The dough is then rolled out into flat rounds using a rolling pin and transferred to a flat pan to roast. To enhance the taste of chapati, it is brushed with pure ghee. The speciality of chapatis is that they can be eaten with spicy curries as well as with sweets.

3. Roti

Roti is a staple in north and central India and is commonly paired with curries, vegetables or dal. It's an integral part of everyday meals. It is a much healthier option as it is made with wheat flour or whole grains. In south india akki roti is made with rice flour and ragi roti is made with finger millet flour.

4. Poori :

Poori is a deep-fried, unleavened flatbread made with whole wheat flour. Pooris are smaller in size. Puffed-up and deep-fried golden pooris are served with potato sabzi or sweets like shrikhand or basundi.

5. Paratha

Parathas are pan-fried Indian flatbreads that are crispy and flaky. They go well with most Indian dishes, be it a gravied curry or a dry stir-fry The more layers you create by folding the dough, the flakier the flatbread will be. North Indians make parathas filled with potato, cauliflower, cabbage, radish or paneer for breakfast and serve them with pickle or yoghurt.

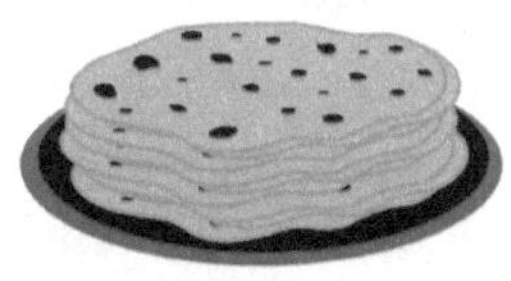

6. Thepla :

Thepla is a spiced wholegrain flatbread from gujarat. Sometimes vegetables like fenugreek leaves are mixed with dough, It is a staple in gujarati households and is eaten with mango pickle or plain curd. Since thepla are spiced & flavour some they can be eaten without any accompaniment or just with masala chai.

7. Kulcha :

Kulcha is typically made of maida or all-purpose flour. While making the dough yoghurt, baking powder, salt, oil/ghee, and water is added to maida. The dough is rolled out into

flat rounds and baked on Tawa.

Amritsar, a city in the state of punjab is famous for kulcha, but amritsari kulcha is quite different. It is a flatbread filled with stuffing like a spicy boiled potato, paneer, cauliflower or onion. With wet hands, kulcha is placed in the hot tandoor.

It is said that the amritsari kulcha recipe was invented by Shah Jahan's royal chef. The king liked the dish so much that he started having amritsari kulcha regularly as breakfast and lunch.

8. Appam

Appam, also known as rice hoppers, are soft, bowl-shaped pancakes prepared with rice, urad dal and fenugreek seeds as the main ingredients. These three ingredients are soaked for a few hours and then ground to a smooth paste by adding coconut milk. This batter is kept for fermentation overnight. At the time of making the appam salt and a pinch of cooking soda are added to the batter.

9. Dosa.

Dosa is a thin, savoury crepe in South Indian cuisine made from a fermented batter of ground urad dal and rice. Dosas are served hot, with chutney and sambar. It's a staple breakfast in many south indian households. There are lots of variations of dosa like masala dosa, set dosa, paper dosa or rava dosa. All 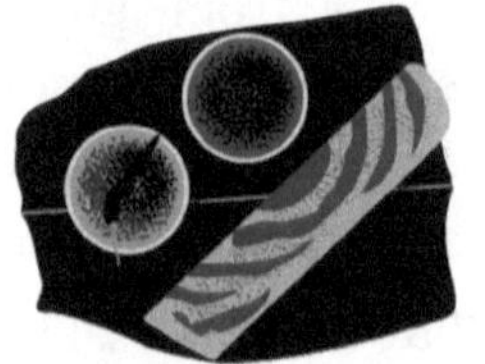 these dosas are popular all over India and abroad.

10. Uttapam

Uttapam is a type of dosa, but it's not crisp. It is soft thick and with toppings like onion, tomato and green chilli. It is served with chutney and sambar.

11. Cheela or Chilla

Cheela or Chilla is an unleavened indian pancake made with lentil or whole-grain flour. The sweet version has jaggery and cardamoms and the savoury version has spices, herbs and vegetables like tomatoes, onion, spinach and fenugreek leaves. It is a healthy and tasty breakfast served with chutney.

12. Bhakri

Bhakri is a healthy flatbread made with millets like jowar, ragi and bajra. It is also made with makai atta (maize or corn flour) or rice flour. Bhakri dough is prepared by mixing flour with hot water and then flattened by hand. It is first roasted on tawa and then on the direct fire. Making bhakri requires a lot of skill. It is commonly found throughout gujarat and rajasthan and their local names differ region-wise.

13. Thalipeeth

Thalipeeth is a savoury multi-grain flatbread popular in the state of maharashtra. The flour for thalipeeth is called bhajani. Chopped onion and coriander leaves are added to the dough, and then patted flat on the griddle. It is shallow fried in a little oil and served hot with fresh butter.

Apart from the types of bread explained above, different Indian states have several other varieties of bread. A few of them are listed below :

- **Maharashtra :** Chapati, Phulka, Bhakri, Puri, Multi-grain

Thalipeeth.

- **Gujarat :** Bajra rotla, Thepla, Khakra
- **South India :** Appam, Dosa, Uttapa, Luchi, Adai
- **Rajasthan :** Bati, Kachori
- **Goa :** Poi, Pao, Katro Pao, Undoo, Kankonn
- **Bengal :** Luchi, Khasta Roti,
- **Punjab :** Tandoor Roti, Roomali Roti, Naan, Laccha Paratha, Kulcha, Makai Ki Roti.

Various Types Of Dals

Dal is a term used for dried, split pulses. The term dal is also used for preparation using the split pulses. In other words, dal has two meanings, Split pulses and Split pulse-based curry.

Dal enhances the taste of Indian meals and provides all kinds of nutrients. It is the staple food of India and is consumed daily in almost all Indian households. Dal is not only tasty but also healthy and nutritious. It is a primary source of protein for many vegetarians.

Indian pulses are usually available in three types.
- Whole pulse.
- Split pulse with the skin on.
- Split pulse with the skin removed.

Indian dal is an easy and very flavourful vegetarian side dish. The most common way of preparing dal is the semi-liquid form to which onions, tomatoes, and various spices are added. This delicious, vegetarian dish is eaten with rotis, chapatis, or with rice.

An interesting thing about dal is that, the same type of dal is cooked in many different ways. Each region of India has its favourite selection of dal and each one is prepared differently.

There are five types of dals commonly used in indian cooking. They are :

1 Toor/ Arhar Dal - Spit Pigeon Peas

2. Masoor Dal – Red Lentils

3. Urad Dal – Split and Skinless Black Lentil

4. Moong dal – Yellow Lentil.

5. Chana dal – Split Chick Peas.

The basic recipe for dal is :

Basic Dal

Ingredients : 1 cup cooked dal (any one or mixture of two or more dals specified above), 1 tomato, 1 tsp of garam masala or 2-3 green chillies, 1 tbsp of chopped coriander leaves. 1 tsp oil, and salt to taste.

Method : Chop tomato. Mash Dal with water. In a pan heat oil and add chillies first then add tomato. Sauté for some time. Add a little water and cook. When the tomato is cooked, add dal mixture. If you are using garam masala instead of chillies then add it at this stage. Add salt. Bring to a boil. Top with chopped coriander.

Here are a few other delicious recipes made with different types of dals.

Moong Dal Khichadi

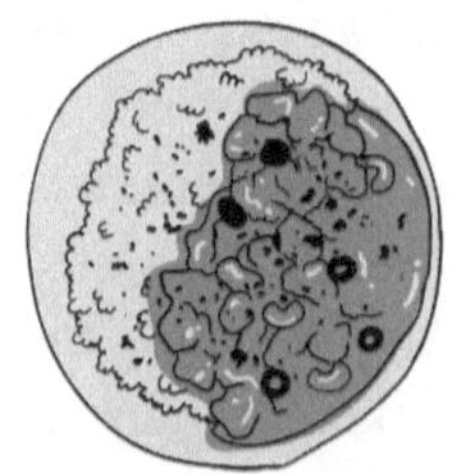

Ingredients : 1 cup small grain Rice, ¾ cup moong dal, 1 tsp coriander powder, 1 tsp cumin powder, 1 tbsp oil, ½ tsp mustard seeds, pinch of asafoetida and turmeric powder, few curry leaves, Salt and chilli powder as per taste.

Method : Rinse rice and moong dal in water. Drain. Heat oil in a pressure cooker and splutter mustard seeds and curry leaves. Add asafoetida, turmeric powder, rice, moong dal and sauté for a minute. Add coriander powder, cumin powder, chilli powder, salt and 4 cups of water and mix well. Pressure cook till 3 whistles. Open the lid after 15/20 minutes. Serve hot with kadhi, papador pickle.

Chana Dal Pakore

Ingredients : 1 cup chana dal, 1 onion and 1 tbsp finely chopped coriander leaves, 1 tsp ginger garlic paste, salt and red chilli powder as per taste, chat masala, oil for frying.

Method : Wash and soak chana dal for 2 to 3 hours. Take it out in a strainer till the entire water is drained. Blend till you get a coarse mixture. Take it out in a bowl. Add onion, coriander, ginger garlic paste, salt and red chilli powder and mix well. Take a spoonful of mixture at a time and fry in hot oil till golden brown. Sprinkle Chat masala and serve with chutney.

Toor dal Rasam

Ingredients : 2 tbsp Toor dal, 2 tomatoes, 1 tbsp tamarind pulp, 2 tbsp rasam powder, 1 tsp oil, a pinch of asafoetida, ½ tsp mustard seeds, ½ tsp turmeric powder, 1 red chilli, 5 to 6 curry leaves and salt to taste.

Method : Put tomatoes in boiling water for 5 minutes. Remove skin and chop. Wash and cook toor dal. In a pressure cooker put dal, chopped tomato, tamarind pulp, turmeric powder, salt and water. Cook till 3 whistles. When cool mash the dal mixture with hand or make a smooth paste in mixer.

In a pan put oil. When hot add mustard seeds, asafoetida, red chilli and curry leaves. When it splutters add rasam masala and dal mixture. Add water and bring to a boil.

Masoor Dal with Pumpkin

Ingredients : 1 cup pumpkin cut into small pieces. 1 cup masoor dal, 1 dry chilli, few curry leaves, 1 tbsp oil, ½ tsp mustard seeds, ½ tsp turmeric powder, pinch of asafoetida, chopped coriander leaves and salt to taste.

Method : Pressure cook masoor dal. Heat oil in a pan and splutter mustard seeds. Add asafoetida, turmeric powder, curry leaves and dry chilli. Add chopped pumpkin, salt and water. Mix well and cook till the pumpkin is soft. Mash masoor dal with some water and add to the pumpkin mixture. Bring to a boil. Add coriander leaves. Serve with plain rice or vegetable pulao.

Sukhi Dal

Ingredients : 1 cup skinned urad dal, 1 large onion chopped, 1 tsp ginger garlic paste, 2 green chillies chopped, 1/2 tsp each garam masala, turmeric powder and amchur powder, a pinch of asafoetida, 1/2 tsp mustard seeds, a handful of fresh mustard leaves, Salt to taste, 1 tbsp mustard oil.

Method : Soak urad dal for half an hour. Heat oil in a pan and splutter mustard seeds. Add asafoetida, turmeric powder, green chillies ginger garlic paste and onion. Sauté and add soaked urad dal with water. Cover and cook till dal is well cooked. Mix with finely chopped mustard leaves, amchur powder and garam masala. Cover and simmer for 5 minutes.

Sukhi dal is a speciality of the state of Punjab. Traditional sukhi dal is made in mustard oil with fresh mustard leaves. We can substitute these 2 ingredients with any other vegetable oil and coriander leaves.

Special Ingredients In Indian Cooking

1. Coconut

Coconut is an essential ingredient in Indian cooking. One of the best things about cooking with coconut is its versatility. This multipurpose fruit is used as the main ingredient in most of the Indian masalas. In southern India, food is cooked in coconut oil. However, in other parts of India, it is used to make curries, garnish for vegetables, chutneys and sweet dishes like barfi and ladoo.

Coconut has acquired a special place in the culture of India. It holds a lot of importance in weddings, festivals, ceremonies or puja. It is a symbol of prosperity and an auspicious object in the ceremony. It is used in many rituals and is offered to deities in temples. Many events and celebrations are inaugurated with the breaking of coconuts.

Almost all parts of the coconut are used in cooking. Coconut meat is the white flesh of a fresh coconut. Coconut milk is made by grating coconut meat and soaking it in water, then squeezing it through a strainer.

Coconut water is typically derived from young green coconuts, which is are freshing and cooling drink.

Shredded coconut comes from dried coconut meat that has been grated or shredded.

There are different ways to enjoy coconut.

Green Coconut Chutney

Ingredients : ½ cup each fresh grated coconut and chopped coriander leaves. 2 green chillies, ½ tsp lemon juice, pinch of sugar, salt to taste.

Method : Put all the ingredients in a grinder bowl and grind till you get a medium coarse texture. Green chutney is used to make delicious sandwiches or can be eaten with snacks like samosa and cutlets.

Bharli Vangi (Stuffed Brinjal)

Ingredients : 8 to 10 small brinjals, 1 cup fresh coconut or 1 cup shredded dried coconut, 1 onion chopped, ½ cup chopped coriander, 1 tbsp sesame seeds, 4 tbsp oil, ¼ tsp turmeric powder, ½ tsp mustard seeds, pinch of asafoetida, 6 to 8 curry leaves, 1 tsp cumin powder, 2 tsps kala / goda masala, jaggery and salt to taste.

Method : Make four lengthwise slits into the brinjals. Heat some oil in a pan and sauté coconut, onion and sesame seeds till golden brown. Cool and grind to a coarse paste. Mix kala/ goda masala, cumin powder, jaggery and salt with the paste. Stuff this masala into brinjals and keep it aside. In a pan heat the remaining oil and splutter mustard seeds and curry leaves. Add asafoetida and turmeric powder. Put stuffed brinjals in the pan and let them coat with the spiced oil. Cover and cook for a few minutes. Gently turn brinjals and cook evenly on all sides. Sprinkle some water, cover the pan and let the brinjals cook on medium flame till well cooked.

2. Yoghurt

Yoghurt or curd is an integral part of Indian food culture. The delicate, mild and milky-flavoured yoghurt is part of every meal in most Indian homes. It is a practice in Indian homes to prepare  fresh yoghurt every day. Traditionally it is set in an earthen pot to get a proper texture.

India is a warm country. If excess milk is not consumed it gets spoiled without refrigeration. From ancient times indians make several other milk products to use the surplus milk. The easiest way was to make curd and then use itfor the next couple of days.

The following is the process of making yoghurt at home.

Home Made Yoghurt

Ingredients : 2 cups milk, 1 tsp pre-made yoghurt or yoghurt culture.

Method : warm the milk. Add pre-made yoghurt and mix well. Pour it in an earthen or ceramic pot. Cover and keep it in a warm place to set. It takes about 8 to 9 hours to set. Yoghurt is ready when it smells pleasantly sour and set.

The bacteria used to make yoghurt are known as yoghurt culture. Fermentation of lactose by these bacteria produces lactic acid, which acts on milk protein to give yoghurt its texture and its characteristic tart flavour.

Yoghurt has created a niche in Indian cuisine and is added to varied recipes to make the dish exotic, unique and flavourful.

Yoghurt is used in many recipes like :

- **Sweets :** Shrikhand, Misti Doi.
- **Curries :** Kadhi, Many vegetable and meat curries.
- **Raita :** A kind of salad made with yoghurt with any one or

combination of boondi (a savoury snack); and vegetables like cucumber, onion, baingan (brinjal), or potato.

- **Beverages :** Buttermilk, Lassi, Masala Chaas.
- **Other dishes :** Curd rice, Dahi Bhalla, Chaat, some Dips, and salad dressings.

Health benefits of yoghurt

- Yoghurt contains a lot of calcium.
- Yoghurt helps in the proper functioning of the digestive system of the body.
- Yoghurt is pro-biotic and helps in developing healthy bacteria in the body. It even reduces bad bacteria in the stomach.

Why do Indians eat so much yoghurt?

- MostIndians are vegetarian, and whole-milk yoghurt contains lots of protein, calcium and fat they need.
- Indians like hot and spicy food. Eating yoghurt with a spicy meal gives a soothing effect.
- Binding the rice or any other dish with yoghurt helps to pick it up and eat it with your fingers.
- Many people are lactose intolerant, and cannot drink milk. Yoghurt is a great substitute for milk.
- Indian chefs use yoghurt to tenderize meat, as a souring agent or as a marinade.
- Yoghurt is ideal to use as a base for lightly textured curries.
- In hot climate regions, yoghurt is supposed tocoolthe body.

Indian dishes made with yoghurt

Dahi Bhendi (Ladyfingers in Yoghurt)

Ingredients : 20 tender and small ladyfingers, 1 cup yoghurt, 1 tbsp besan, ½ tsp each cumin seeds, coriander powder and ginger paste, 1 red chilli, 1 tbsp oil, salt and sugar to taste. Coriander leaves for garnish.

Method : Trim the stem and tip of the ladyfingers. Whisk yoghurt and add besan, coriander powder, salt, sugar and a little water. Mix well. Heat oil in a nonstick pan and splutter cumin seeds. Add ginger paste and red chilli and sauté. Add lady fingers and cook on a medium flame for 3 to 4 minutes. Add yoghurt mixture and cook until ladies' fingers are well cooked. Garnish with coriander leaves and serve.

Chicken Dahiwala

Ingredients : ½ kg boneless chicken, 1 cup yoghurt, 2 tbsp ghee, 2 onions, 2 tbsp ginger garlic paste, turmeric powder, 1 tsp, cumin powder, 1 tsp garam masala, Chilli powder and salt as per taste. 1 tbsp chopped coriander leaves and 10 cashew nuts for garnishing.

Method : Chop onions finely. In a large bowl mix together yoghurt, turmeric powder, cumin powder and salt. Marinate chicken pieces in this mixture for 30 minutes. Heat ghee in a pan and fry cashew nuts. Take them out and in the same pan sauté chopped onion till golden brown. Add garam masala, ginger garlic paste and sauté. Add marinated chicken and mix well. Cover and simmer for 15 minutes. If needed sprinkle some water. When chicken is cooked mix chopped coriander leaves. Garnish with fried cashew nuts and serve hot with paratha.

Vegetable Raita

Ingredients : 1 white onion, 1 small tomato, 1 cucumber, 1 green chilli, 1 tbsp chopped coriander, 1cup yoghurt, a pinch of cumin powder, salt to taste.

Method : Cut green chilli into 2 pieces. Chop onion finely. Cut the tomato and take out the pulp. Peel cucumber. Chop tomato and cucumber finely and mix with chopped onion. Whisk yoghurt and mix with cumin powder, salt coriander leaves and chilli. Add chopped vegetables and mix well.

3. Besan

Besan means gram flour. It is made by grinding Bengal gram or Chana dal. Besan is a popular ingredient used in Indian cooking. It is also commonly used as a replacement for eggs in vegetarian cooking. 

- Besan makes a tasty and crispy coating fordeep-fried snacks.
- Besan is used exclusively as a main ingredient in a variety of dishes.
- Besan is used as a thickener for gravies.
- Besan is used as a binding agent in many dishes.
- Besan is used as the main ingredient while making zunka, gatte, Besan Chilla, Boondi, Fafda, Shev, Khandvi, and Dhokla.

However, it is also used as a secondary ingredient while making a variety of snacks and sweet dishes. The following are a few examples.

- **Snacks :** Potato Vada, Vegetable Pakora, Besan Puri.
- **Sweets :** Besan laddoo, Motichoor, Mohanthal, Mysore Pak.
- **Binding agent :** Kothimbir Vadi, Kabab, Kofta, Tomato Omelette.

Zunka

Ingredients : 2 tbsp oil, 1 tsp each mustard and cumin, a pinch of asafoetida, ¼ tsp Turmeric powder, 4 clove garlic, 1 chilli and 1 onion finely chopped, 1 cup besan, 2 tbsp coriander leaves chopped, salt to taste and water as required.

Method : In a large kadhai heat oil and roast besan for two minutes. Take it out and keep it aside. In the same kadhai splutter mustard and cumin. Add asafoetida and chopped onion, garlic and chilli. Sauté on low flame. Mix roasted besan, turmeric and salt with water. Pour over the onion mixture. Cover and simmer for 10 minutes, or until besan is cooked completely. Sprinkle some water and mix well. Finally, add in coriander leaves and enjoy zunka with bhakri.

Tomato Omelette

Ingredients : 1 cup gram flour, 2 tomatoes and 1 onion finely chopped 1 tsp ginger, garlic and green chilli paste, 1 tbsp chopped coriander, pinch of turmeric powder, salt to taste water as required and oil.

Method : In a bowl put all the above ingredients and water. Mix well to make a thick pouring consistency batter. Heat a flat pan and add1 tsp of oil. Pour the batter into the pan and spread it to make a round. Cover and let it cook on law flame. Flip and cook the other side. Both sides should be browned. Serve with chutney or tomato sauce.

4. Kokum

Kokum is a tropical summer fruit which is packed with flavour and various health benefits. The outer cover of fruit is dried in the sun and such dried cover is called *amsul*. It is used in curries, chutneys, and pickles  as a souring agent. It grows mainly in the states of maharashtra, goa, karnataka and kerala.

The fresh fruit is preserved with sugar to make bright-red squash, which is diluted with water to make a beverage called kokum sarbat. It is a popular summer drink in India which is often consumed to prevent dehydration. The refreshing drink is believed to cool down the body and prevent heat stroke.

Ingredients : 1 large Coconut grated, 15 amsul, 5 garlic cloves, 2 green chillies, 3-4 cups water, salt and sugar to taste.

Method : Soak the amsul in 1 cup of hot water for 45 minutes. Put the grated coconut, chillis and garlic in a blender with 1 cup of water. Grind for 30-45 seconds. Sieve the coconut mixture to get the thick first press of coconut milk. Repeat the process to get a thinner second press. Mix the thick coconut milk with the amsul water. amsul is very sour, so add sugar and thin coconut milk as per taste. Add salt and mix well. Serve chilled or at room temperature.

5. Amchur Powder

Amchur means Mango powder. It is made from dried unripe green mango and is used as a citrusy seasoning. It gives a nice flavour to the food.

It is added to several popular Punjabi dishes like Chole, Rajma, and Aloo Paratha to get that tangy flavour. In north Indian cuisine amchur is used as a souring agent instead of lime tamarind or kokum.

Unripe mangoes are cut into strips and dried in sunlight for a couple of days or until they become crisp. dried mango strips are ground into fine powder.

Amchur Aloo

Ingredients : 6 medium-sized boiled potatoes. 1 tbsp amchur powder, 1 tbsp oil, 2 green chillis, 1" ginger chopped, 1 tbsp chopped coriander leaves. ¼ tsp each garam masala and cumin powder, Salt to taste.

Method : Chop potatoes into cubes. Heat oil in a pan and sauté ginger and chillis. Add chopped aloo and cook for some time.

Sprinkle amchur powder and garnish with chopped coriander leaves.

Sweet and Sour Chutney

Ingredients : ½ cup grated jaggery, 2 tbsp amchur powder, 1 tsp cummin powder, ½ tsp chilli powder and salt to taste.

Method : Put all the ingredients in a pan. Add ½ cup of water and cook on a low flame until all the ingredients are dissolved and mixed well. Cook till chutney thickens.

Indian Beverages

1. Filter Coffee

Filter coffee or filter kappi is a cultural icon of south india. South indian filter coffee is a strong, milky coffee decoction served in a traditional dabarahand tumbler. Making perfect decoction for tasty filter coffee is considered an art.

The coffee filter consists of two cups, one that nests on top of the other. The upper cup holds the coffee grounds, and it has holes that let the brew drip into the lower cup. The strong decoction is collected in the lower cup. There is also a pressing disc for tamping the grounds and a lid for keeping the decoction warm while brewing.

Coffee is drunk from the tumbler, but first, it is cooled with a dabarah. Dabrah is a wide metal saucer with lipped edges. Once the coffee is brewed; it's poured back and forth between a dabarahand tumbler in fast arc-like motions of the hand.

Pouring the coffee between the tumbler and the dabarah serves several purposes :

1. Mixing the sugar and coffee thoroughly.
2. Cooling the hot coffee to a sipping temperature.
3. Creating the frothy layer over the filter coffee.

Roasted and ground chicory is added to the coffee powder which gives filter coffee its aroma and colour. Normally the ratio is 80% coffee to 20% chicory. The chicory holds on to the hot water a little longer, letting the water dissolve and extract more of the coffee ground.

Spices used in the Filter Coffee

Spiced coffee is enjoyed in most parts of india. It is a flavourful, rich, creamy and frothy coffee, which is a perfect blend of spices and coffee. Adding a pinch of spice to the coffee grounds can enhance its taste. Here are a few spices commonly used in coffee.

1. Cardamom when added to the coffee, cardamom holds up well to the coffee's fruity bitterness.
2. Cinnamon gives a nice smell and flavour and is a delicious addition to hot beverages like coffee.
3. Nutmeg gives a slightly sweet and unique smell to the coffee.
4. Ginger Adding a few slices of ginger to the coffee grounds before brewing gives the perfect taste to the coffee. If fresh ginger is not available, dry ginger powder can be used.

Spiced Coffee Brew

It's very easy to make spiced coffee at home. In a coffee filter, add coffee, cardamom, cinnamon and nutmeg powder. Mix gently with a spoon to combine. You can use any combination of spices of your choice. Add water to the coffee maker and brew.

Ingredients : 3 tsp freshly ground coffee powder. ½ cup boiling water, ¾ cup milk, 2 tsp sugar.

Method : To make the perfect decoction, take a traditional South Indian coffee filter. Put the coffee powder in the top perforated container of the coffee filter and place the stemmed pressing disc over it. Place this container over the bottom part. Pour boiling water into the upper container. Cover and keep for 15 to 20 minutes. Thick decoction will be ready.

To make a filter coffee, pour ¼ cup of decoction into a tumbler and add boiling milk on top. Add sugar. Mix well by pouring coffee back and forth between the tumbler and the dabarah. Delicious filter coffee is ready.

2. Chai (Indian Tea)

Tea is one of the most popular hot beverages in the world. A cup of tea in the morning gives us a refreshing feel. Recipes of teavary across continents, cultures, towns and families.

Tea is an integral part of Indian culture. There is no single occasion in our country which is complete without a cup of tea. India is the second largest producer of tea in the world after china. Teacame to india from china but was popularised largely in the british colonial era when large plantations were established.

The speciality of Indian tea is adding different spices to the tea. It's called masala chai. **Chai** is a Hindi word for tea. The spices used in tea vary from region to region. The most common spices are cardamom, cinnamon, cloves, and pepper. Some people add herbs like lemongrass, mint or ginger tothe tea for an extra kick.

Chai

Ingredients : 2 cups water, 1 cup milk, 2 tsps tea powder, 2 tsps or more sugar as per taste.

Method : Boil water in a saucepan. Add sugar and tea powder in it and boil it for 3-4 minutes on medium flame. Add milk and boil it over medium flame until the bubble starts to rise. When the colour of the tea changes from milky to brown, it is ready. Turn off the gas and strain the tea into cups.

Chai Masala

The secret of a great cup of chai is the spice mixture called chai masala.

Method 1 : In a mixing bowl combine 1 tsp cinnamon powder, ½ tsp cardamom powder, ½ tsp ginger powder, ¼ tsp ground cloves and ¼ tsp nutmeg powder. Mix well and store in an airtight container.

Method 2 : Put 3" piece of cinnamon, 4 cardamoms peeled, and 6 cloves in a mortar. Crush and grind them with a pestle to powder. Strain and mix with ½ tsp ginger powder. Mix well and store in an airtight container.

Chai Walas of India

In India, a chaiwala is a person who prepares, sells and serves tea on streets or small roadside shops. They are an integral part of Indian tea culture. Traditionally, tea was made in brass vessels. Chaiwalas boil a mixture of water, milk and tea leaves in a big vessel and then strain it into a tea kettle. They

usually serve tea in small glasses or clay tea cups called kulhad.

Chai walas are everywhere from busy street corners, small lanes, bus stands, and railway platforms, near parks and temples. They even walk through the train cars. When you need a hot cup of tea, the chai wala is always near. Making chai is what chaiwalas do for their living, so they take pride in their chai. Many chai walas develop their own style of preparing and presenting chai.

Cutting Chai

Cutting chai translates to 'cut into half', which means a small quantity of tea. The term cutting chai originated in mumbai for half a cup of tea. It is less in quantity and price but just enough to refresh your senses.

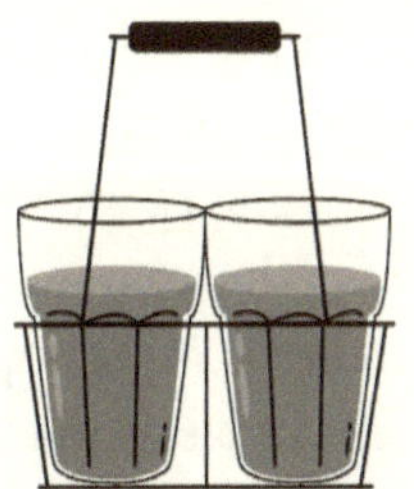

A 'cutting chai' in one hand and a 'vada pav' in the other hand is how most people in mumbai start their day.

Irani Chai

Irani cafes are iranian-style cafes in India. They were started by iranian immigrants to british india in the 19th century. They found out that the locals preferred their tea with lots of milk and sugar, so they invented their own recipe for the tea and soon it became popular as irani chai.

Irani chai is a unique form of tea made by adding mawa or khoya to black tea. The result is a sweet and creamy chai. The spices like cinnamon and green cardamom are also added to this chai. The exact ratios of these ingredients of irani chai is a secret closely held by most Irani café owners.

3. Lassi

Lassi is a traditional yoghurt-based drink, which is very popular all over India with some variations and different names. Basic lassi is a blend of yoghurt, water, sugar or salt. It is also made with a blend of spices, fruits, dry fruits and nuts.

Drinking cold and refreshing Lassi is an old tradition for Indians. India has been a land of milk. Thus, lassi is the staple diet in villages and is consumed to maintain good health and keep fit. This easy-to-make and inexpensive drink is drunk year-round but is most popular during the summer. Following are the variants of lassis made in india.

Salted Lassi

Ingredients : ½ cup ice-cold water, ¼ tsp salt, ½ cup home made yoghurt, pinch of cumin powder.
Method : Blend yoghurt, salt, cumin powder and water. When the mixture is frothy pour it in glass.

Sweet Lassi

Ingredients : ½ cup cold water, 2 tsp sugar, ½ cup home made yoghurt and few ice cubes.
Method : Blend yoghurt, sugar, ice cubes and water. When the mixture is frothy pour it in glass.

Masala Chaas

Ingredients : 1 cup plain yoghurt, 2 cups cold water, 1/2 tsp grated ginger, 1 tbsp chopped coriander leaves, 1/2 tsp cumin powder, salt to taste, (1 green chilli and ¼ tsp chat masala-optional,) few mint leaves for garnish.
Method : Blend yoghurt, water, grated ginger, coriander leaves,

cumin powder and salt till well mixed. Pour in a glass and garnish with mint leaves.

Masala chaas can made in advance and kept in the refrigerator. It tastes best when chilled.

4. Other Indian Beverages

Apart from tea, coffee and lassi, each state of india has its own famous drink. They are tasty and healthy. In india, there is a drink for every season. Cool and Sour drinks for summer and hot beverages for monsoon and winter.

Sugarcane Juice

Sugarcane juice is the liquid extracted from pressed sugarcane. It is consumed as a beverage in many places, especially where sugarcane is grown in plenty. Fresh lime juice and salt are added to  the sweet juice to make it tastier and is served with crushed ice.

Kokum Sorbet

Kokum sorbet is a refreshing beverage from the states of goa and maharashtra and it is made to beat the scorching summer heat. It is made with soaked dry kokum, cumin, black salt and sugar. This delicious sorbet has many health benefits.

Aam Panha

Aam Panha is the first choice of people in summer. It is made from unripe mangoes, sugar, cardamom powder and saffron. It helps to maintain body temperature in summer and is a perfect drink to beat the heat! 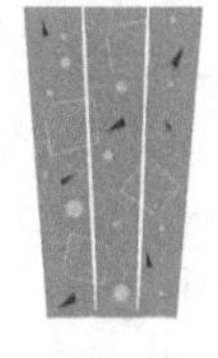 

Nimbu pani

Nimbu Pani is simple lemon water or lemonade. Indian lemonade is made by mixing lemon juice, sugar, salt and water. It is the most sought-after summer drink to beat the heat.

Kahwa

Kahwa is a kashmiri tea flavoured with cinnamon, cardamom, and saffron. It is a great drink to sip on cold winter days. Kahwa is traditionally prepared in a brass kettle known as Samovar by boiling tea leaves along with saffron, cardamom pods, cinnamon sticks and some locally available dried fruits.

Kahwa has several health benefits too. It aids in digestion, improves metabolism, is a remedy to colds, increases immunity and is a stress buster.

Jal Jeera

Jal jeera is a popular summer drink in India. It consists of cumin, ginger, black pepper, mint, and black salt. This tangy, sour, aromatic and spicy drink is very healthy and refreshing.

Thandai

Thandai is a traditional drink, made during the festival of colours, holi and is popular in the northern parts of india. The main composition of this beverage is a sweetened mix of nuts, seeds and a few spices, which forms a paste. Almonds, pistachio, cashew nuts, poppy seeds melon seeds are

soaked in milk and then ground to make a paste. This paste is then diluted with milk which makes a refreshing drink thandai.

Falooda

Falooda is a mixture of many ingredients such as milk, jelly cubes, ice cream, rose syrup, vermicelli, and ice cream. After a spicy meal, the consumption of falooda makes digestion easy and cools the body.

Uses Of Leaves In Indian Kitchen

From the time humans lived in forests, different kinds of leaves have been used for various reasons. They are not edible but have an important role in the kitchen. The leaves are excellent casing that protects the food from being exposed to direct heat and prevents dirt or fluids from seeping in. They protect and preserve the juices released from food during the cooking process. Leaves also trap some steam and seal in the flavours, allowing the food to cook in mellow heat in its juices. The results are fantastic.

Over time, through trial and error, cooks learnt to identify leaves that were not merely a protective casing but also added flavour and sometimes medicinal properties to the food. In Indian culture, different varieties of leaves like banana, turmeric, sal, jackfruit and lotus leaves are used in the kitchen. These leaves help in almost every culinary process like steaming, baking, grilling, and cooking.

Leaves give an extra flavour to the food cooked in it. In south india, plain idlis are made special and fragrant by steaming idli batter in jackfruit leaves, banana leaves or turmeric leaves.

Broad and dried leaves of Sal or jackfruit are used to make *Patravali*, an indian eating plate. It is made in a circular shape, by stitching 6 to 8 leaves with tiny wooden sticks. It was a custom to serve food on a *Patravali* during traditional meals, festivals and in temples.

1. Curry Leaves

Curry leaves are natural flavouring agents which give Indian food a pleasant aroma and enhance its taste. They give a nice flavour to vegetables, curries, soups, rice dishes and dals.
Curry leaves are usually stripped from the stem and fried in hot oil with other spices. It is used as a base for making a dish or to pour over an already-made dish for flavour. They are edible after they are cooked so there is no need to remove them before eating.

Curry Leaves Chutney

Ingredients : 1 cup curry leaves, 1 tbsp shredded dry coconut, 1 tbsp sesame seeds, 4 dry red chillies, 1 tsp oil, salt and sugar to taste.

Method : Fry curry leaves in oil till crisp. In the same pan roast coconut, sesame seeds and dry chillies till crisp. Grind curry leaves, sesame seeds, coconut, chillies, salt and sugar to make a fine powder. Put in an airtight container.

2. Turmeric Leaves

The turmeric plant is widely known for its edible roots, but all parts of this plant including the leaves and flowers are edible. Turmeric leaves are fragrant and they impart their heavenly aroma and flavour to the food cooked in them.
With the onset of monsoons, turmeric leaves grow in

abundance. They are used as a wrapper for steamed dishes. The famous turmeric leaf dish made in goa and konkan is *Patholi*. It is a sweet dish made with sweetened coconut and rice flour dumplings steamed in turmeric leaves. Small pieces of turmeric leaves are also used in curries, chutneys, or to make pickles. Some chicken and fish dishes are cooked in turmeric leaves. They protect the spices from burning and seal the flavours. Cooked meat remains juicy and tender with a nice smoke flavour of turmeric leaves.

Sweet Pangi

Pangi is a healthy and tasty Maharashtrian snack. Traditional sweet pangi is made at the time of Ganesh Chaturthi festival.

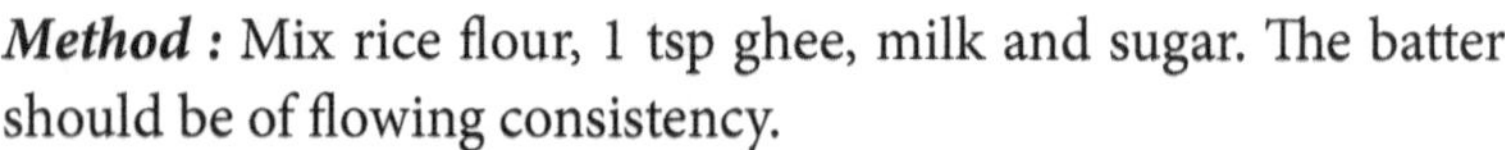

Ingredients : 2 cups rice flour, 4 tsp ghee, 2 cup milk, 3 tbsp sugar, turmeric leaves.

Method : Mix rice flour, 1 tsp ghee, milk and sugar. The batter should be of flowing consistency.

If required add some water. Keep aside for 15 minutes. Heat the pan. Grease turmeric leaf with ghee and put it on the pan with greased side up. Spread 2 tbsp batter on the leaf evenly. Cover it with another greased leaf and press gently. Cover and cook *Pangi* on both sides till the brown spots appear on the turmeric leaf.

Health benefits of turmeric leaves.

1. Crushed turmeric leaves help to digest the food.
2. Turmeric leaves have strong anti-inflammatory and anti-bacterial properties.
3. The paste of turmeric leaves helps to keep the skin soft, smooth and glowing.

3. Banana Leaves

Banana leaves are dark green coloured, large and broad in shape. The use of banana leaves in the kitchen is not new. The practice of eating food on a clean banana leaf is an old tradition. Eating food on banana leaves is considered healthy and auspicious. As they are big enough to serve a multi-course meal, they are used to serve authentic indian dishes at festivals.

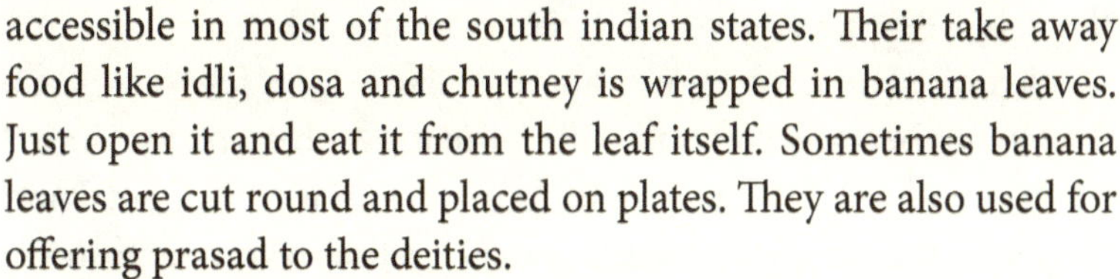

Owing to the abundance of banana trees around, banana leaves were easily accessible in most of the south indian states. Their take away food like idli, dosa and chutney is wrapped in banana leaves. Just open it and eat it from the leaf itself. Sometimes banana leaves are cut round and placed on plates. They are also used for offering prasad to the deities.

Advantages of using the banana leaves

1. Banana leaves have anti-bacterial properties that help to protect the food from being ruined by germs or bacteria.
2. Banana leaves are eco-friendly.
3. Banana leaves have a wax-like coating that prevents dirt and dust from sticking tothe surface of the leaf.
4. Serving food on banana leaves is one of the most economical and inexpensive options.
5. When food is cooked in the banana leaf, it imparts its smell to the food and improves the taste and flavour of that dish.

Some famous and tasty Indian dishes are made in banana leaves.

Patra Ni Macchi

Patra Ni Macchi is a famous parsi dish. It literally means fish wrapped in banana leaves. It's a healthy alternative to the fried fish.

Ingredients : 2 medium-sized pomfret, ½ tsp turmeric powder, 1 cup coriander Leaves, 1 cup mint leaves, 5 green chillies, 8 cloves garlic, ½ tsp cumin powder, ½ cup fresh coconut grated, 1 tsp lemon juice, salt to taste and banana leaf to wrap the fish.

Method : Clean the fish and make small slits on both sides. Rub salt and turmeric powder into the slits. Make green chutney by grinding coriander leaves, mint, green chillies, garlic, cumin powder, coconut and salt. Apply this chutney on both sides of the fish. Keep covered for 15 to 20 minutes.

Heat the banana leaf over an open flame for a few secondsso that it will become soft and will not tear. Cut banana leaf into 2 squares and pot fish on it. Fold four sides to make a parcel and tie it with thread. Place the fish parcels in the steamer and steam for 10 minutes. Cut the thread and serve fish.

We can also cook the tied parcel in a microwave oven or on barbeque or shallow fry on a griddle.

Panki

Panki is a gujarati dish made by cooking rice batter between banana leaves. It can be made with different ingredients like moong dal flour, oats, gram flour or soya flour. To make the *pankis* healthy we can add spinach, sesame seeds, shredded carrot or green peas to the batter. Traditional Panki is made with a mixture of rice and urad dal flour.

Ingredients : 1 cup rice flour, 1 tbsp urad dal flour, 1 tbsp curd, pinch of cumin powder, chilli paste, salt as per taste, 1 tsp oil and banana leaves.

Method : Combine rice flour, urad dal flour, curd, cumin powder, chilli paste, salt and oil. Mix well by adding water. Cut banana leaves into circles of 4" diameter. Grease them with oil. Spread 1 tbsp batter on each circle and cover it with another circle. Heat a little oil on a nonstick pan and cook *panki* on both sides till the brown spots appear on the banana leaf. Serve hot with green chutney.

4. Betel Leaves (Paan)

Chewing a paan after a mealisan ancient Indian tradition. Some buy it at nearby paan shops or some make it at home. Betel leaf plays an important role in Indian traditions, customs and rituals and is one of the important items in pooja or other religious ceremonies. They are considered a symbol of prosperity.

Eating betel leafis considered very healthy. All you need to do is to chew a few betel leaves on an empty stomach.

Health Benefits of Betel Leaves
1. It acts as a breath freshener.
2. It is good for diabetes. calcium rich.
3. It helps to lower the cholesterol levels.
4. It helps in healing wounds.
5. It improves oral health.

The most common dish made with betel leaves is a Paan. Let's see a few more recipes made with the betel leaves.

Home made Paan with Gulkand

Ingredients : 6 Betel leaves, sweet fennel seeds, 1 tsp gulkand*, 1 tsp powdered betel nut (supari), 1 tsp desiccated coconut, Chuna**, pinch of Paan Masala and 6 cherries.

Method : Clean and dry betel leaves. On the light side of the leaf, slightly spread the chuna and make a cone. Once the cone is ready fill it up with gulkand, supari, desiccated coconut and paan masala. Close the cone and insert a toothpick and cherry in the middle. Repeat it for the remaining betel leaves.

Gulkand is a sweet preserve of rose petals

**Chuna* is Calcium Carbonate

Paan Milk Shake

Ingredients : 5 Betel leaves, 2 cups milk, 3 tsp gulkand, pinch of cardamom powder, sugar to taste, few ice cubes.

Method : Wash and chop the betel leaves. In a blender mix together betel leaves, milk, cardamom powder, gulkand, sugar and ice cubes. Blend till the mixture is smooth. Strain and pour into glasses. Serve chilled.

Paan Smoothie

Ingredients : 5 betel leaves, 5 spinach leaves, a few mint leaves, 1 apple, 1 tbsp yoghurt, a pinch of salt, Sugar to taste.

Method : chop betel leaves and spinach leaves. Peel and cut the apple into cubes. Put betel leaves, spinach leaves, mint leaves, yoghurt, apple, salt, and sugar in a blender. Blend to make a smooth drink by adding a little water.

5. Lotus Leaves

Lotus leaves play a significant role in indian culinary traditions. In some states of india, they are used for cooking, storing and packing food. The water-repelling property of the lotus leaves keeps the food fresh. Eating on lotus leaves prevents the food from sticking to them. Apart from this, they are rich in antioxidants and can help enhance the flavour of your food. They are mostly used to serve the Prasad.

6. Jackfruit Leaves

Jackfruit leaves are another type of leaf that is rich in antioxidants. You can steam and wrap the food inside them. When the steam touches the leaves, it releases essential nutrients that get absorbed into the food.

These leaves are mainly used in South Indian cuisine to enhance flavour. Jackfruit leaves are pre-dominantly used for steaming, especially as a wrapping for sticky rice cakes and steaming idlis.

Using these leaves not only has cultural significance but also contributes to your health, making them ideal for serving food.

Popular Indian Dishes

India is a famous tourist destination for travellers all over the world. Visiting India is a dream for most people because of its rich heritage, culture, historical landmarks and unique cuisine. Lip-smacking, spicy and tasty indian food is one of the main factors to attract tourists from all over the world. Here is a selection of some popular indian dishes.

1. Dal Tadka

Dal Tadka is a lentil dish made with toor or *arhar dal* (pigeon pea) or *masoor dal*. It is a staple food of many Indians which is typically served with either rice or chapati. The secret of tasty dal tadka is the base of onions and tomatoes followed by the tempering of ghee, red chilli, mustard seeds and asafoetida. It is very popular among vegetarians.

2. Paneer

Paneer is an Indian cheese that's made from curdled milk and some sort of fruit or vegetable acid like lemon juice. It's made quickly, typically within an

hour or two, and has the unique property of not melting when heated.

3. Koftas

Koftas are round balls made from ground meat, mashed vegetables or paneer. The grounds are mixed with herbs and spices and deep-fried. Different types of curries are prepared with these koftas. They are also used in biryanis and rice.

4. Papad

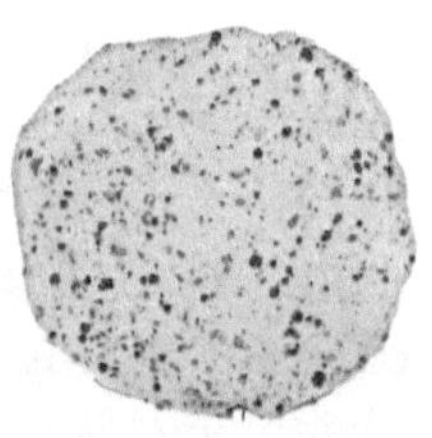

Papad is a crispy flatbread or wafer. It is always served as a side dish. They are deep-fried or roasted over an open flame. Papad recipes vary from region to region and from household to household. They are typically made from a dough made with chickpea flour, black gram flour, rice flour or potatoes. An Indian thali is not complete without it.

5. Dosa

Dosa is a traditional south indian dish. This thin and crispy pancake is made from fermented batter of soaked rice and lentils. It is usually stuffed with potato sabji and served with chutney and sambar.

With its huge popularity, there are many variations of dosas, such as mysore masala, rava masala, onion masala, ghee roast and paper masala dosa. It is usually consumed as a quick snack or as a part of any meal of the day.

6. Pakoras

Pakoras means fried fritters. Pieces of vegetables like potatoes, onions, cauliflower, green chilli or chicken are dipped in a spiced batter of chickpea flour and deep fried. Pakoras are enjoyed as an appetizer or snack.

7. Korma

Korma is a style of curry that is slow-cooked in a thick mild gravy made with cream, coconut milk and cashew-almond paste. It's delicately spiced with coriander, saffron, ginger, cardamom and black peppercorn. Kurma is usually served with puri.

8. Khichadi

Khichadi is one of the health and comfort foods made with a combination of rice and moong dal. Across India, khichdi recipes are made in different ways, but the basic ingredients and combinations remain the same. Generally, it has all spices and flavours in it and is served as it is, It tastes great when served with kadhi, pickle or creamy yoghurt.

9. Chole Bhature

Rich, spicy and heavy, Chole Bhature is a popular punjabi dish. This heavenly combination of white chickpeas masala is served with soft and fluffy deep-fried Bhature, onion and lemon. This sumptuous dish can be found at  most street carts in north india and is best enjoyed on an empty stomach!

10. Mango Lassi

Mango lassi is a popular lassi variety, made with curd, sweet mango, sugar and cardamom powder. Mango lassi is the perfect chilled drink for hot summer months when the fruit is in season.

11. Kulfi

Kulfi is a frozen dairy dessert that comes in exotic flavours. It is a 'traditional Indian ice cream'. which is commonly sold by kulfiwallahs (a vendor selling kulfi).

Kulfi is denser and creamier than ice cream. The density of kulfi causes it to melt more slowly than ice cream.

12. Mutter Paneer

Mutter paneer is a north indian curry made with cubes of paneer. Peas and paneer are cooked in tomato and onion-based sauce.

Thalis Of India

Thali is a traditional Indian meal which is every traveller's dream. Thali means a round plate. Thali is used to serve food in the Indian sub continent. Thali is an Indian-style meal of various dishes which are served on one plate. Thali is often called a feast on a plate. Thali is acultural exploration.

Indians are known for having elaborate meals. Thali is a combination of small amounts of numerous dishes served in small bowls, lined inside a large plate. Different types of vegetables, dal, snacks, rice, roti, meat, chutney, pickle, papad and dessert are served in a thali. Indian thali is the perfect assortment of delicious regional dishes on a single platter. Authentic local restaurants serve vegetarian and non-vegetarian thali. There can be many dishes served on a thali plate, it usually ranges between nine to sometimes even twenty-five dishes.

From a nutritional point of view, Indian thali is a balanced meal providing carbs, protein, vitamins, minerals, and fibre. Dairy, which also plays an important role in Indian cuisine, is used in the form of ghee, curd and buttermilk to make the Indian thali wholesome.

Various cooking techniques like steaming, poaching, shallow frying, roasting, grilling, deep frying and dry roasting are used in Indian cooking, and most of them are used when composing a thali.

Each Indian state has its own thali and as you move from one region to another, you'll be welcomed with a new platter, with its own elaborate menu. Most thalis serve local and seasonal food. Indian thali is a complete representation of six tastes (sweet, sour, salty, spicy, bitter and astringent), which are essential for a balanced meal and a balanced body.

Since ancient times, one of the ways for the rich to show off their wealth was through the variety of food cooked in their kitchens. In those days thalis were made of silver with five to six matching bowls and glasses. Silverware brimming with neatly arranged, colourful and steaming hot food makes thali highly photogenic.

In modern times, silver thalis are used for religious offerings and for serving food during wedding functions. Steel thalis are for everyday use in homes and restaurants.

Thali is not necessarily only vegetarian. In the coastal regions of India, there are variations of fish and sea food thalis. In other parts of the country, you will find different types of mutton and chicken thalis. These thalis with its array of colours and is a feast for our eyes. Each thali is named after the dish in which it is traditionally served. Each of them celebrates their region along with its delicacies.

Here are some of the Indian thalis that are nothing less than a grand feast.

1. Bengal Thali

Bengali Thali is a feast for fish lovers. Most of the dishes are cooked in mustard oil which gives a special taste and flavour to the food. It includes signature delicacies like the pan-fried brinjal, bottle gourd curry, shaak, cholar dal, luchi, fish fry, fish curry, mutton in thick gravy and sweets like *rasgulla, rasmalai* or *payesh.*

Shaak is green leafy vegetables.

Cholar Dal is a traditional Bengali dish prepared with chana dal, ghee, coconut and spices and is best paired with luchi or steamed rice.

2. Goan Thali

Goa is famous for fish curry and rice. Goan thali is also seafood lover's favourite thali. It includes boiled rice, fish curry, pork vindaloo, mackerel fry, steamed cabbage vegetables, kismur, Pao and sol kadi. Special goan sweets like bebinca or dodol are served at the end.

- **Kismur** is a salad of fresh or dry grated coconut and fried dry prawns
- **Sol kadhi** is a drink made with kokum-coconut milk.
- **Pao** is goan bread.

3. Kashmir Thali

Kashmir is a paradise for meat-lovers as many popular dishes *rogan josh, gushta baandyakhni* are meat-based. Rogan Josh is the signature dish of the valley. The ultimate ceremonial feast in kashmir is known as *Wazwan* and its preparation is an art in itself.

The kashmiri cuisine is very rich and healthy. Their thali includes kashmiri pulao, khatte baingan, rajma, nadru kebab, goshtaba, dum aloo, vegetable raita with walnuts, kebab, mutton rogan josh, yakhni and pickles. The thali is served along with different traditional loaves of bread. The feast ends with phirni, flavoured with rose and saffron.

4. Maharashtrian Thali

Thali from maharashtra showcases the traditional staples of the state. It ranges from mild to very spicy lip-smacking delicacies. This thali includes rice, bhakri, potato sabji, *amti, pithale, kothimbir wadi*, black-eyed beans curry, chicken in white gravy, mutton kolhapuri, raita and sweets like kheer or puran poli.

- **Amti is** Spicy sweet and sour toor dal
- **Pithale** is thick chickpea flour curry
- **Kothimbir wadi** is a coriander cutlet

5. Punjabi Thali

Punjab is famous for tandoor and rich food. Punjabi thali is a lot like its people – rich, robust and full of life. It includes pieces of breadlike Nann oraloo *kulcha*, *kadhi-pakore*, *pindi-chole*, shahi-paneer, jeera rice, dal makhani and lassi. The non-vegetarian delicacies in the thali can be butter chicken or amritsari fish.

- **Pindi chole** is spicy chickpea curry.

6. Himachal Pradesh Thali

Dhaam is a traditional thali of himachal pradesh. The dish includes dal, rajma, rice, curd, boor ki Kadi and is very well complemented with jaggery.

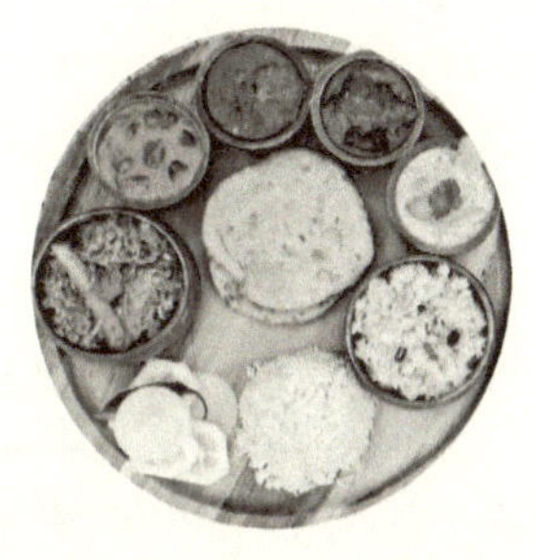

Dhaam is a plate full of delicious delicacies that are a must-serve on occasions and festivals. The distinctive feature ofthis dish is that it is prepared by special chefs known as 'botis'. To grab the best taste of *Dhaam* you must visit himachal during festivals.

The traditional *Dham* is served on plates made of leaves. Traditionally the *Dham* is cooked on firewood instead of cooking gas. *Dham* is a mid-day meal served on the occasions of marriage, birthday party, retirement party or any religious day.

7. Kerala Thali

A traditional kerala thali is called *Sadhya. Onam Sadhya* looks quite appealing to the eyes because it is served on green banana leaves. Typical Sadhya includes items like rice, dal, two dry vegetables, one wet vegetable, sambhar and rasam, fried papad, raita,  vada, banana chips, *payasam*, curd, buttermilk, fresh pickles and chutneys. Families would sit cross-legged on the floor and eat with their hands.

8. Rajasthan Thali

The traditional Rajasthani Thali is rich, colourful and regal just like its culture. *Dal Bati* and *Gatte ki Sabzi* adorn the plate along with the roti made of bajra, makka, and jowar. It also includes panchmela dal, kersangri, boondi chaas, pulao or bajra khichadi and papad. Laal maas and mohanmaas are Rajasthan special non-vegetarian dishes. For dessert, there is moong dal halwa, balushahi or mohanthal. All in all, it is a gastronomic delight

- **Gatte** is gram flour balls.

9. Gujrat Thali

Gujarat Thali is a vegetarian's paradise. It includes flatbreads like rotla, thepla, and puris and some *farsans* or snacks like samosas or dhokla. Main entrees include dal, dal dhokla, dry vegetables, curry, undhiyu, kadhi khichdi and buttermilk. All these dishes are on  the sweeter side as it is common to add jaggery to food. Some delicious desserts include doodhpak and jalebi. Additionally, gujarati thali also has certain seasonal sweets, for example, aamraas (kind of a mango juice) is served during the summer.

- **Undhiyu** is a traditional mixed vegetable dish.

10. Andhra Thali

Since the state has a long coastline, the cuisine has a lot of seafood. The food is very spicy witha variety of curries, chutneys and pickles. Vegetarian Andhra thali consists of rice served with ghee, chapati or puri, sambar, rasam, fried and wet curries, dry sabji  of bitter guard and ivy guard, medu vada, sabudana papad, chutney, pachadi and yoghurt. Andhra people are rice lovers, so there is a variety of rice dishes like biryanis, lemon rice, and tamarind rice.

In andhra pradesh, there are numerous traditional sweets like *khaja, besan laddoo, payasam* and sweet poli.

In India, it is said that 'All the thalis from different regions connect people through the language of food, and this language does not need any words but just feelings and love.'

Chaat

Chaat, is a traditional savoury snack sold by street vendors in India that originated in the country's northern region. This hidden treasure of India is now popular worldwide. It is said that chaat was created in the kitchens of mughal emperor shah jahan.

The rich culinary diversity of India has led to the creation of chaat dishes inspired by its various regions. While each may look and taste a little different, they all share a common combination of sweet, salty, crunchy, spicy and savourying redients. Even if chaat is considered a snack, it can be eaten at any time of day.

Though Chaat originated in Uttar Pradesh, it became popular as an appetizing snack all over India. People from different states use different ingredients while making chaat. In the states of Gujarat and Rajasthan chick pea flour is used while in Punjab and Uttar Pradesh, wheat flour and lentils are used. In some places people use puffed rice; but in Mumbai, we can taste a blend of all these.

Chaat is mostly served at roadside carts and stalls. It usually includes ingredients like shev, papadis, boiled potatoes, tamarind chutney, mint chutney, puffed rice, small puries, yoghurt and onions. These ingredients are mixed in different combinations to produce different chaat delicacies.

These are some of the famous chaat dishes.

1. Bhel Puri
2. Dahi Puri
3. Sev Puri
4. Ragda Pattice
5. Papdi Chaat
6. Pani Puri
7. Dahi Vada
8. Alo tikki
9. Samosa chaat
10. Papdi chaat
11. Raj kachori
12. Basket Chaat

All chaat dishes have a solid foundation, like aloo tiki, Samosas, puffed rice, crispy puris or sprouts. Vegetables like onions and tomatoes; which are used raw and boiled potatoes are the next key ingredient of chaat which gives texture to the dish. Chaat is completed with any one or a combination of any of the sweet, spicy and tangy chutneys. They are as follows :

- **Tamarind Chutney :** This classic Indian chutney is sweet, sour and spicy. It's made from tamarind pulp, spices and a sweetener like sugar, jaggery or dates.
- **Red Chutney :** This fiery sauce is made with garlic, spices and ground red chillies.
- **Mint Chutney :** This chutney is made with cilantro, mint, garlic, cumin and chillies. It is spicy but refreshing.

After chutney comes a healthy dusting of chaat masala and black salt. The addition of coriander powder, cumin powder and red chilli powder is as per personal taste.

- **Crispy Topping :** Finally comes the crunch. No chaat dish is complete without something crispy and fried on top. Popular toppings include savoury **Sev, fried potato or boondi.**

Sev means deep-fried noodles made from chickpea flour.

Boondi means deep-fried balls made from chickpea flour.

While each ingredient of chaat is relatively simple but turns into a tasty and tangy magic dish when combined.

Papdi Chaat

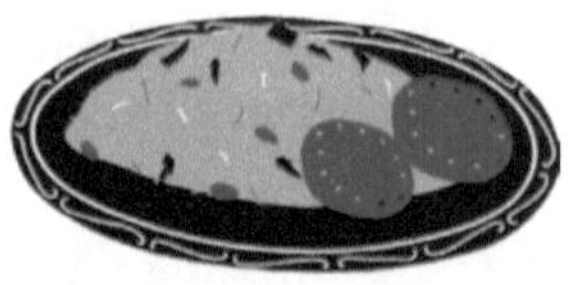

Ingredients : 15 small crisp puris(Papdi), 2 potatoes boiled and chopped, 2 onions finely chopped, 1 tomato finely chopped, 1 cup chickpeas boiled in salted water, 1 cup curd whisked. 3 tsps each Geen chutney and tamarind chutney, 1 cup sev, pinch of chilli powder, cumin powder and chat masala, coriander leaves for garnishing and salt to taste.

Method : In a serving dish arrange Papadis. Top each papdi with potato and chick peas. Sprinkle chopped onion and tomato over papdis. Drizzle whisked curd over it. Put green chutney and tamarind chutney on top. Sprinkle chat masala, chilli powder, cumin powder and salt. Top with sev and garnish papdi chaat with coriander leaves.

Aloo Tikki Chaat

This recipe has two steps, first Aloo Tikkis are made and then the aloo tikki chaat is made using such tikkis.

For Aloo Tikki-

Ingredients : 3 medium size potatoes, ½ cup bread crumbs, ½ cup fresh peas, ½ tsp garam masala, ½ cup chopped coriander and salt to taste. Oil for shallow frying.

Method : Cook potatoes and peas. When cool mash the potatoes without any lumps. Add boiled peas, garam masala, bread crumbs, coriander and salt. Mix well to form a smooth dough.

Divide the dough into six portions. Make balls and flatten them. Heat a pan and drizzle the oil. Put aloo tikkis on the pan and shallow fry them on both sides till they turn golden brown and slightly crisp.

For Aloo Tikki chaat -

Ingredients : Six Aloo tikkis. 3 tbsp sweet and sour tamarind chutney. 2 tbsp hot green chutney, 1 medium size onion finely chopped, ½ tsp red chilli powder and pinch of chat masala and salt, ½ cup sev and chopped coriander leaves.

Method : Arrange aloo tikkies in a flat dish. Put some onion on each tikki and top with tamarind chutney and green chutney. Sprinkle salt and chat masala and sev. Finish with coriander leaves and serve.

Mumbai Street Food

Mumbai, the City of Dreams, the City that never sleeps, the financial capital of India, New York of India, Foodies' paradise. Mumbai is known by many such names. It is a glorious mixture of cultures, people and food.

From authentic indian cuisine to world-class delicacies, and affordable street food to high-end eateries, mumbai offers several options. Street food in mumbai is a foodie's delight. The culinary richness is visible in the form of street food with gujarati, south indian, parsi, and maharashtrian influences. There are numerous stalls at every corner of the city, selling varieties of reliable, quick and cheap food.

When in mumbai you should pamper your test buds with authentic delicacies and exciting street food. Mumbai is something you should experience and see with your own eyes.

Mumbai's most popular street food is made with Pav. When the portuguese invaded goa they brought various types of dishes with them. The bread which was called pao was one of them. The *Goan pao* is unique as it is baked in wood-fired mud ovens. This bread is called pao because the bakers kneaded the dough with their feet.

In maharashtra, this bread is called Paav or Pav, with almost the same pronunciation. It is a local derivative of the word Pao. All the words, Pav or Paav or Pao in the context of food mean the same i. e. the leavened bread.

Ladi pav comprises three or four rows of pav merged, arranged in slabs or "ladi". It is a common food item in Mumbai and is used in many recipes, especially roadside snacks likemisal pav, pav bhaji, masala pav, vada pav, maska pav, burji pav and kacchidabeli. Even snacks like kanda bhaji and samosas are accompanied by pav. Many working-class people start their day with a pair of pav and tea.

1. Misal Pav

Misal pav is a speciality of maharashtra. It is made using usal, a curry of sprouted moth beans (Matki) and thin oily rassa. Rassa is a spicy and hot gravy. Two more ingredients in misal are poha and farsan, salty and crunchy Indian snacks.

To serve misal : Put some pohas at the bottom and put freshly chopped tomatoes, onions, and plenty of farsan (fried savoury combination) on it. Farsan gives texture to the dish. Cover it with hot gravy and serve. Misal is always accompanied by pav. It is generally served as a breakfast or as an evening snack.

2. Masala Pav

A mixture of potatoes, finely chopped onion and tomatoes is slightly sautéed with spices, coriander and sometimes pav-bhaji masala. This mixture is stuffed between the sliced pav which is roasted on tawa with loads of butter.

It is garnished with chopped coriander and shev.

3. Vada Pav

Everyone's favourite Vada pav or the poor man's burger is among the top mumbai street foods. The recipe of vada pav is hard to duplicate because each stall owner has his own secret ingredients. If you visit mumbai and you do not experience vada pav, your trip is incomplete. The following is the recipe for vada pav.

Vada Pav

Ingredients for vada : 2 potatoes, 1 green chilli, 2 cloves of garlic, one-inch piece of ginger, 2 tsps oil, 1/4 tsp mustard seeds, few curry leaves, a pinch of turmeric powder, pinch of asafoetida and salt to taste.

Ingredientsfor coating : 1 cup besan (gram flour), 1/4 tsp turmeric powder, 1/4 tsp red chilli powder or to taste, a pinch of baking soda, salt to taste and oil for deep frying.

Other ingredients : 6 pav, green chillies, green chutney and dry garlic chutney.

Method : Boil potatoes until tender. When cool, mash them coarsely. Grind green chillies, garlic and ginger together. Heat oil and add mustard seeds and curry leaves. When the mustard seeds splutter, add the chilli-garlic-ginger paste and fry for some time. Add mashed potatoes, turmeric powder and salt. Turn off the flame and mix well until the mixture is well combined. Make 6 balls/vadas with this mixture.

Mix besan, turmeric powder, red chilli powder, baking soda, and salt in a bowl. Add enough water to make a thick paste. Dip vadas into the besan mixture and fry in hot oil until golden brown. Once all the vadas are done, fry 2-3 green chillies in the same oil.

To assemble the vada pav place green chutney on one side of the pav. Put potato vada on it and top off with dry garlic chutney. Serve with fried green chillies.

4. Pav Bhaji

Pav Bhaji is a speciality dish from the by-lanes of mumbai. It is an indian fast food made of steamed and mashed vegetables like potatoes, cauliflower, peas, tomatoes and onions. They are further cooked in special pav bhaji masala and loads of butter. It is eaten with shallow fried pav. It is said that the origin of pav bhaji is mumbai which was a quick and light meal for the mumbai mill workers. The following is the recipe for pav bhaji :

Pav Bhaji

Ingredients : 3 potatoes peeled and cubed, 1 cup cauliflower cut into big pieces, 2" piece of beetroot, peas - ½ cup, 1 onion finely chopped, 1 capsicum finely chopped, 4 tomatoes finely chopped, 1 tbsp ginger garlic paste, 4 tbsp butter, salt to taste, chopped coriander leaves and 2 tsps pav bhaji masala, ½ tsp lemon juice and chopped coriander leaves.

Method : Put potato, cauli flower, beetroot and peas in a pressure cooker with some water and cook for 3 whistles. Turn off the heat and let the steam go all by itself. Open the cooker and mash the veggies roughly with a masher, Set aside. Melt butter in a kadhai and sauté onions, tomatoes and capsicum. Cook till golden brown. Add ginger garlic paste, and salt. Add mashed vegetables and Pav Bhaji masala and mix well. Add some water and simmer for a few minutes. Till then the pav bhaji gravy thickens. Remove from the flame and finish with lemon juice and coriander leaves.

To serve pav bhaji-

Heat a spoonful of butter on tawa. Cut open a pav and toast for a minute till golden brown. Remove to a plate.

Add a spoonful of butter on the same tawa and add some bhaji on it. Mix well and cook till it is thick. Transfer this to the plate. Dollop some butter on top and serve with sliced onions and lemon.

5. Pav Samosa

Samosa is a fried snack with a savoury filling like spiced potatoes, onion, peas or meat. Samosas are very popular and commonly eaten snacksacross India. They are flaky and crispy from the outside with tasty potato and peas or kheema stuffing inside. Lovingly shaped into triangles and deep fried, these calorie busters are the best bites during a Mumbai monsoon.

6. Kheema Pav

Kheema Pav is a signature Parsi/ Irani dish eaten at breakfast, lunch, and dinner. Kheema is a spicy mutton mince cooked with spices, onion and tomato. It isserved with pav and is thus called Kheema Pav. In some places, pav is toasted on a pan with lots of butter and stuffed with delicious kheema. It is served with onions, roasted green chillies and lemon.

Buttered pav and spicy kheema are one of Mumbai's iconic street foods. The kheema pav recipe is said to have originated in Irani restaurants in Bombay. Today it is found everywhere from old parsi eating joints to new cafes and five-star hotels.

7. Paneer / Egg Bhurji Sandwich

This Sandwich is packed with bhurji which is protein-rich paneer or eggs scrambled together with Indian spices and herbs. Pav is slit and layered with lettuce, tomatoes, onions and bhurji. Bhurji sandwich is a simple and filling snack.

8. Usal Pav

Usal Pav is a traditional and delicious maharashtrian street food served in mumbai. Usal is made, using sprouted white peas with tangy tomatoes and tamarind. Usal pav is accompanied by toasted pav, finely chopped onions, sev and green chillies.

9. Kacchi Dabeli

Dabeli means 'pressed' in gujarati language, which is implied by the way this dish is prepared. This dish originated in the Kutch region in gujrat so it is called kachchi dabeli.

Dabeli Masala is the key ingredient of the dabeli recipe. This masala is mixed with boiled and mashed potatoes and saluted onions and then stuffed or pressed between buttered pav. The pav is sliced into two parts. Green chutney is spread on one slice of the pav and the potato mixture is pressed on it. It is topped with fresh pomegranate, fried peanuts and chopped onions and covered with the other half slice of the pav. It is topped with lots of sev or shev.

10. Kanda Bhaji with Pav

The deep-fried onion pakoras are stuffed in between pav with green chutney and hot garlic chutney. Typically onion pakoras is an ideal snack which can be easily served also as a meal. Sometimes Potato or green chili pakoras are also served with pav. Bhaji pav is enjoyed with a hot cup of chai.

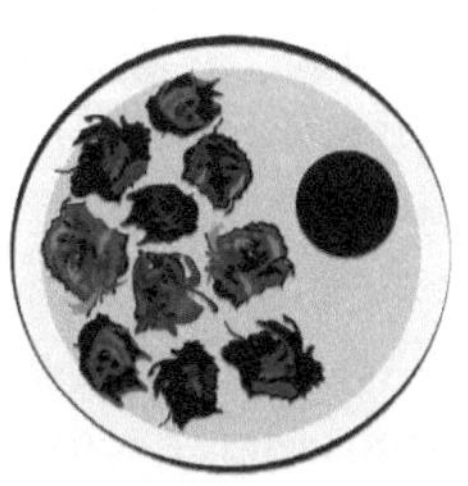

Signature Cuisines of Indian States

Food plays an important role in Indian culture. In India, food and culture go hand in hand. Diversity in soil, climate, cultures, festivals and traditions present in India are reflected in the food. Every regionhas their specialities and different ways of cooking. In every Indian state, food is prepared uniquely, using spices and recipes native to that region.

Every indian state has its unique culinary traditions. The range of food items that one can explore in India is extensive and diverse. Every indian state has hundreds of great dishes that make it special. Most of the Indian cuisines are vegetarian; but indian people love non-vegetarian delicacies like fish, chicken, mutton and other meats. Tasting and gathering knowledge about regional food gives us a chance to explore the culinary traditions of our country.

Delhi, mumbai, kolkata, goa and kerala are on the bucket list of every foodie traveller. They get attracted to these places to experience the food which is unique, full of flavours and as diverse as the land itself. Delicious recipes of these Indian states will surely awaken your taste buds.

Delhi & North India

Rich, aromatic and spicy vegetables, moist and tender meat and desserts form unique North-Indian cuisine. It is influenced by the moghul style of cooking in which curries geta thick, moderately spicy and creamy texture. Dairy products like milk, cream, cottage cheese, ghee and yoghurt play an important role in the cooking of both savoury and sweet dishes. A variety of fruits and vegetables is available at all times of the year; thus, this region produces a dazzling array of vegetarian dishes.

Delhi is considered the food capital of India. It has a mixture of ancient indian and mughal-styled cuisine. From street food to fine dining, delhi has something to offer everyone. The top street food of delhi is chaat, kebab, chole bhature, jalebis, falooda, samosa, kathi roll and kulfi. However, the iconic dish of delhi is biriyani served in earthen pots.

Wheat is a main ingredient in north indian meals. Punjab is called the bread basket of india. Parathas, Naans, Roti, Kulcha, Bhatura, Puri and Kulcha are some of the flat breads made in Punjab. Parathas with different kinds of vegetarian and non-vegetarian fillings is a speciality of north india. Parathas are called the king of breakfast. They are served with butter, pickle or curd in every other house from ages.

Cooking in the tandoor is traditionally associated with Punjab. Tandoor is a clay oven used to cook Punjabi food and food cooked in tandoor is called tandoori. Marinated meat is cooked over an intense fire in a tandoor. Tandoori chicken, chicken tikka, paneer tikka, naan, and amritsari kulchaare a few of the famous tandoori dishes.

Butter chicken is known as the 'pride of Punjab,' . Marinated chicken is cooked in a tandoor before being served in a rich, spiced tomato and butter sauce. Vegetarian versions of this dish can also be found on Indian restaurant menus with paneer instead of chicken.

Malai Kofta, dal makhani and rajma are very popular among vegetarians. Koftas are small balls made with fresh paneer and vegetables and then dipped in a rich creamy sauce. In dal makhani dal is cooked with dollops of cream and butter, giving it a rich and mouth-watering taste. Rajma is a lightly spiced, creamy and delicious curry made with kidney beans, onions, ginger, garlic, spices and tangy tomatoes. Makkeki roti and sarsonka saag, a typical punjabi dish, where corn roti is served with curry made with leafy green vegetables.

Meat dishes like kebabs and biryanis have a special place in north indian cuisine. Kebabs are one of the best things the Mughals left behind. Lucknowis a famous place for kebabs. From seekh to shami, galouti to kakori, there's one for every type of foodie. These kebabs are succulent pieces of meat marinated in aromatic indian spices and grilled to perfection.

Another speciality of lucknow is biryani, which is cooked in dumpukth style. This makes the biryani juicy and aromatic.

Here are a few mouth-watering recipes from north India.

Galouti Kababs

Galouti means 'which melts in the mouth'. There is an interesting legend behind these kababs. They were specially prepared for a Nawab of Lucknow who had lost his teeth but wanted to eat meat. In order to please him, mouth-watering kababs were made in his royal kitchen. Nawab loved  those soft and tender kababs which literally melted in his mouth. Thus, born the galauti kababs.

Ingredients : 500 gm mince meat, 2 tsp raw papaya paste, 3 tsp ginger-garlic paste, 1 large onion sliced, 2 tbsp ghee, 2 tbsp yoghurt, 1 tsp red chilli powder, 1/2 tsp garam masala, I tbsp gram flour, ½ tsp cardamom powder, Salt to taste. A few drops of kewra water (optional).

Method : Wash mince meat in a sieve and allow the water to drip off. Put it in a bowl and add salt, papaya paste and ginger garlic paste. Mix the mixture well and keep aside for 20-30 minutes. Hang the yoghurt until the water has drained out. Fry onion in ghee till crisp and golden brown. Crush onion and mix with hung yoghurt. Add this to the minced meat along with red chilli powder, gram flour and garam masala. Divide the mixture into six portions and shape into round patties. Place a thick or non-stick tawa on fire and add some ghee. Fry the mince patties on both sides till they are cooked to a golden-brown colour. Serve hot with onion rings, green chutney and lemon.

Rajma

Ingredients : 1 cup red kidney bean, 2 bay leaves and salt to taste. Soak rajma for 8 to 10 hours. In a pressure cooker put soaked rajma along with 3 cups of water, bay leaves and salt. Pressure cook till rajma is well cooked. Keep aside cooked rajma and water.

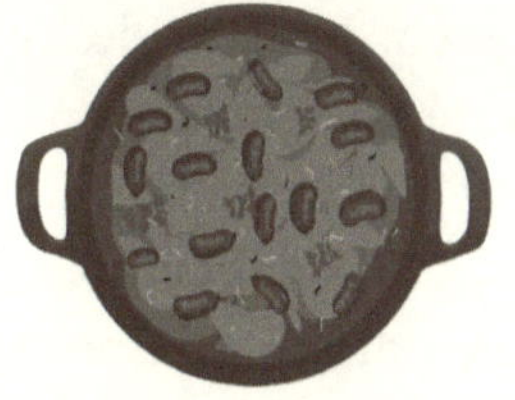

Masala : 2 onions, 3 tomatoes, ½ cup fresh coriander, 2 tbsps ghee, 1 tbsp ginger garlic paste, 1 tsp cumin powder, 1 tsp garam masala, 1 tsp red chilli powder, a pinch of turmeric powder and a pinch of asafoetida. Salt to taste.

Method : Chop onions and tomatoes. Heat 1 tbsp of ghee in a pan and sauté onion until golden brown. Add ginger-garlic paste, and tomatoes and fry for a minute. Take out and keep aside. When the mixture is cooled put it in a mixer and make a smooth paste. Put the remaining ghee in a pan and fry this paste along with turmeric powder, red chilli powder, garam masala, coriander powder and cumin powder. Cook until the ghee separates from the masala. Transfer cooked rajma with water to the masala. Mix well. Add salt and simmer for about 5 minutes. Garnish with fresh coriander leaves and serve with rice.

Carrot Halwa

This popular north indian dessert is made with carrots, milk, khoya and dry fruits. It is one of the simplest indian desserts which is appreciated not only in India but across the globe.

Ingredients : 1 kg carrot, ¼ cup ghee, ½ cup chopped cashew nuts and almonds, 3 cups milk, 1 cup sugar, ½ cup khoya, ¼ tsp cardamom powder and a pinch of saffron.

Method : Peel the skin of carrots and grate finely. Keep aside. In a thick bottom panheat ghee and fry dry fruits till golden brown. Keep aside. In the same ghee add grated carrots and sauté for 5 minutes or until it changes colour slightly. Add milk and stir well. Boil until the carrots are cooked well. Once the milk thickens completely, add sugar. Mix well and cook until the sugar dissolves. Cook until the halwa thickens and ghee releases from the sides. Turn off the flame and add crumbled khoya, cardamom powder, saffron and fried nuts. Mix well.

Kolkata and East India

Kolkata is the capital city of the state of west bengal and is nick named as 'city of joy,' 'city of palaces,' and 'gateway of eastern India.' Kolkata is known for its diversified food culture, a wide range of cuisines and varied cooking techniques. Bengali cuisine is very popular for itsaromatic taste and delicious flavours.

Fish is an integral part of bengali cuisine. Kolkata offers a wide variety of fish preparations. The main course is generally fish served with rice. The fish is either fried, or cooked in gravy. The most common fish varieties used in Kolkata are hilsa, rohu, and catla. Kolkata is renowned for its Hilsa fish, which is considered a delicacy in the region. This oily, flavourful fish is typically prepared in various ways like frying, steaming, or curries. Bhetki Fish (Asian Seabass) is another popular fish in kolkata known for its firm, white flesh. It is often fried and served with mustard sauce or cooked in curry. Creamy coconut milk-based Shrimp curry is a signature dish of kolkata.

Macher jhol (Fish curry) is a famous Bengali spicy fish curry. It consists of chunks or slices of fish that are slowly simmered in a flavourful broth. The curry is prepared with onions, turmeric, chilli peppers, grated ginger, coriander, nigella seeds, cumin, and mustard seeds.

Bengalis are known for their love of food. After fish, different types of dal and many vegetables like bitter gourd, pumpkin, brinjal, onion, and beans are important parts of Bengali cuisine. Aloo poshto is an old traditional delicacy which is served as a side dish in every Bengali household. Made of poppy seeds and potato, is the perfect side dish with dal and white rice, shukto, vegetables mixed in ginger and mustard sauce, chutney or kasundi (mustard sauce), and papad.

Pachphoran is the key element of tasty Bengal food. While making tempering for any dish, five spices- Cumin seeds, Nigella seeds, Fennel seeds, Wild celery seeds and Fenugreek seeds are used. The flavour and aroma of pachphoran is so potent that we don't need to add other aromatics like onions, garlic, or ginger to the dish.

When we think of Bengali cuisine, the rich aroma of mustard oil inevitably comes to mind. Mustard Oil, with its sharp, pungent flavour, is more than just an ingredient; it's a symbol of heritage and tradition. Beyond the kitchen, mustard oil is used in religious ceremonies and rituals.

Street food is one of the major characteristics of Kolkata. It includes Indian, as well as Chinese, Mughlai, British and Nepali foods. Kolkata Street food includes Momos, Phuchka, Ghugni and Singara chaat, Masala Kachori, Aloo Kabli, Jal Muri, Kathi Roll and Badam Makha.

Gol Gappas and Paani Puri, these tiny water bombs with spicy masala and methi chutney are one of the best things to have in the streets of Kolkata. Another Kolkata street food is Jhalmuri. Puffed rice or muri is mixed with peanuts, coriander and other spices, which make it an appetizing quick bite. When in Kolkata one cant miss Kathi Rolls. They are mostly made like a flaky flour paratha, which is further rolled up with egg, mutton, chicken, paneer or vegetable stuffing and is laced with irresistible sauces, spices, and chutney.

Luchi is a classic Bengali flatbread, which is prepared with maida flour. It resembles the famous North Indian bhatura or Puri. Luchi is served alongside Aloo Posto or any other rich Bengali curry!

Bengal is known for its delicious varieties of sweets. Bengal sweets are mostly made of chhena (cottage cheese). Sweets like Sandesh, Chenar Jalebi, Cham Cham, Pantua and Rasmalai are a few of the Bengali sweets made from chhena. King of Bengali sweets is the Rosogolla. Small balls are made of chhena and are dipped in a sweet syrup. These soft, spongy, and syrup-soaked delights are a must-try for anyone with a sweet tooth.

Mishti Doi

The creamy and delectable Mishti Doi is one of Bengal's most well-known and well-liked desserts. It is made with a mixture of thick milk and jaggery or caramelised sugar.

Ingredients : 4 cups full cream milk, 3 tbsp jaggery or 4 tbsp sugar, 3 tsp yoghurt.

Method : Boil milk on medium flame till it thickens and reduces to half. Meanwhile put sugar in a pan along with a little water. On a medium flame stir it till sugar caramelises. Mix caramelised sugar into boiled milk. Stir and allow the mixture to cool. If you are using jaggery mix it with milk and boil the mixture till jaggery dissolves. Transfer milk to a clay pot and mix yoghurt. Stir well. Cover and allow it to set in a warm place for seven hours or till it sets completely. Refrigerate for two hours and garnish with chopped nuts.

Macher Paturi

In Bengal, Patra Fish is called Macher Paturi. Macher means fish and Paturi means leaf. Fish like Hilsa, Bhekti or rohu are used in this Bengali dish. Fish pieces marinated in a spiced mustard paste are wrapped in 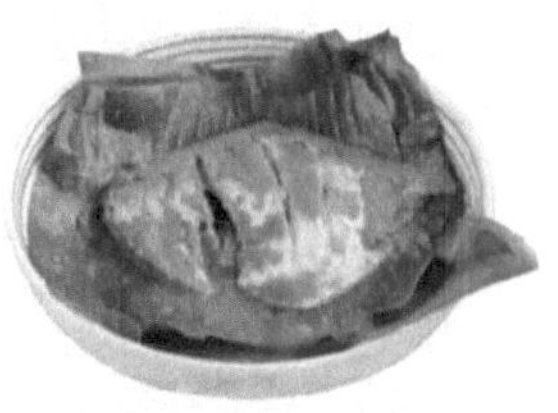 banana leaf individually and then slow cooked till tender. The basic Macher Paturi marinade has just ground mustard, green chillies, turmeric, mustard oil and salt. The pungency of the mustard is toned down with coconut and poppy seeds.

Ingredients : 4 Bekti fillets, 2 tbsp mustard seeds, 1 tbsp poppy seeds, 1/4 cup fresh coconut grated, 4 green chillies, 1 tsp turmeric powder, salt to taste, 2 tbsp mustard oil and banana leaf.

Method : Apply salt and turmeric powder to the fish fillets. Grind mustard seeds, poppy seeds, green chillies and coconut to a smooth paste by adding a little water. Marinate fish pieces in this paste and keep covered for half an hour.

Warm the banana leaf over an open flame for a few seconds so that it will become soft. Cut it into 4 squares and apply some oil toit. Put the fish piece on the banana leaf and fold it to make a parcel. Tie the parcels with thread. Heat oil in a pan and put fish parcels on it. Cover the pan and let the fish cook on a medium heat on both sides. Serve it with rice.

Aloo Posto

Aloo Posto means potatoes cooked in a paste of spiced poppy seeds. Poppy seeds, mustard oil and nigella seeds used in Posto cannot be substituted with any other ingredient.

Ingredients : 3 tbsps white poppy seeds (soaked overnight), 2 large potatoes, 2 tbsps mustard oil, ½ tsp nigella seeds (kalonji), 3 green chillies, salt to taste and water as required.

Method : Drain all the water from soaked poppy seeds. Put them in a chutney grinder. Add 1 green chilli and some water and Grind to a fine paste. Cut the potatoes into square pieces. Heat mustard oil in a pan and add nigella seeds. Sauté the nigella seeds for a few seconds. Add chopped potatoes. Mix the potatoes evenly with the mustard oil and nigella seeds. Sauté the potatoes, until they are half cooked. Add the poppy seeds paste and two whole green chillies. Season with salt and mix again. Cover the pan with a lid and on a low heat simmer till all the water dries up and the potatoes are cooked. The consistency should be dry and there should be no water in the pan. The poppy seeds paste will coat the potatoes. Aloo Posto should be dry to semi-dry.

GOA

Goa, India's smallest state by are a islocated in the western region on the coastline of the Arabian Sea. Colourful architecture, lush greenery and breath taking beaches are the real beauty of Goa. The 103-kilometre coastline of Goa is blessed with some of the most beautiful beaches. Each beach has a different vibe and attracts a different kind of traveller. For many tourists, Goa is a paradise on earth.

Goa was a Portuguese colony before 1961, and hence, food in Goa is a perfect blend of Portuguese and Indian culture. Goan dishes are adaptations of traditional Portuguese dishes using local Goan ingredients. Goan cuisine is dominated by seafood which includes shark, tuna, pomfret, prawns and mackerel. The staple food of Goa is rice and fish curry. Most of the dishes incorporate coconut, rice, fish, pork, meat and local spices.

The most iconic dish in the list of traditional Goan cuisine is Pork Vindhalo. Vin comes from the word vinegar and aloh means garlic inthe Portuguese language. The main ingredients in vindhalo are pork, vinegar and garlic along with onions, red chillies, and spices. Goan people added potatoes (Aloo) to vindhalo and called it vindaloo. Whatever the name, the final result is red hot gravy with pork.

Recheado is another Portuguese-influenced dish. Recheado means 'stuffed' in Portuguese language. This dish consists of fish stuffed with tangy masala and onions and served with warm Goan bread.

Bebinca is one of the most famous and loved desserts in Goa. It is a multi-layered cake that is prepared using coconut milk, sugar, eggs and flour. Caramelised sugar gives the dessert a rich flavour.

Feni is a local alcoholic drink with a strong aroma. The word Feni derives from the word Fenn which means froth. When Feni is poured in a glass it produces a little froth, which is an indication of the superior quality of the product. The two most popular types of Feni are cashew Feni and coconut Feni.

Tangy Balchao, spicy Vindaloo, flavorful Cafreal and much loved Xacuti are the four famous Goan curries.

Fish Recheado

Recheado masala is a red paste which is used in cooking, Mackerel, Pomfret, Prawns or Kingfish.

Ingredients : 4 slices of kingfish, 15 Dry Red Chillies, 1/2 tsp Cumin, 8 cloves, 2-inch Cinnamon stick, ¼ tsp Peppercorns, 12 Garlic cloves, 1 Onion Sliced, 2 ½ tbsp Vinegar, 1 tbsp  Oil, ¼ tsp turmeric powder, ½ tspsalt and pinch of sugar.

Method : Soak spices in vinegar for two hours. Heat oil and fry the onion for two minutes. Grind spices and onion to a fine paste. Add salt, turmeric powder, sugar and vinegar as per taste. The recheado masala has to be thick.

Coat the fish slices with this paste and keep aside for at least 30 minutes. Heat oil in a pan and shallow fry the fish. If you want it to be crispy coat the fish with semolina or rice flour. Fry for 3 - 4 minutes on both sides.

Serve the Fish Recheado with lemon wedges.

Grilled Mackerel or Pomfret with Recheado Masala.
Make slits on each side of the fish with a sharp knife. Coat the fish with Recheado paste and keep aside for at least 30 minutes.

Heat the grill and oil the grill grates. Put the marinated fish on the grill and cook over medium heat for about 4 to 5 minutes per side or until done. Remove from grill and serve with sautéed vegetables.

Chicken Cafreal

This spicy chicken in green gravy originated in the beautiful country of Mozambique, and was introduced
to Goa by Portuguese. Whole Chicken legs are marinated with lots of coriander leaves, ginger, garlic, lime juice and spices.

Ingredients : 6 Chicken Legs, Juice of one lemon, Salt to taste.
Rub the chicken legs with lemon juice and salt. Cover and keep aside.

Green Masala : 1 large bunch of Coriander, 2 tsps each of Pepper Powder and Cumin Powder, 1 tsp each of Turmeric Powder, Poppy Seeds, Cinnamon Powder, 8 Cloves, 4 Green Chillies. 3" pieces of Ginger, 15 flakes of garlic, 1 tsp Tamarind pulp and sugar to taste. Put all the ingredients in a mixer jar along with a little water and make a smooth paste.

Method : Coat chicken pieces with green paste and keep aside for 5 to 6 hours. In a heavy bottom kadhai heat oil and add marinated chicken along with the marinade. Stir well. On a low flame simmer chicken for twenty minutes. Add a splash of water if it gets too dry. Chicken Carfreal is a dry dish. When chicken is cooked add vinegar to taste and cook for 5 minutes.

Sannas

Sannas are spongy steamed rice cakes of Goa. They are made from a batter consisting of ground red rice and

freshly grated coconut. The rice and coconut are ground using Toddy (fermented coconut water.) The batter is then fermented and steamed in moulds.

There are two types of Sannas, Plain and Sweet. Sweet Sannas are filled with cooked coconut and jaggery mix.

Plain Sannas are a popular accompaniment for sorpotel, xacuti, fish curry, and other spicy meat curries.

Ingredients : 1 cup Parboiled Rice, ½ cup grated Coconut. 1 cup Coconut Toddy, pinch of Sugar, Salt to taste. Oil to grease the moulds.

Method : Wash and soak rice overnight. Next day, drain and grind it with ½ cup toddy for a few seconds. Then add another ½ cup of the toddy, sugar, and salt and grind till you get a coarse paste. Add gratedcoconut and grind for a few seconds.

Transfer to a bowl and keep covered in a warm place for 5 to 6 hours. Let the batter ferment till it has almost doubled.

Grease the moulds with oil and fill them with the batter. Place moulds in the steamer and steam for 15 to 20 minutes or till done. Demould the sannas and serve with hot and spicy Goan curry.

Kerala and South India

Kerala means Land of Coconut Trees. It is known for beaches with coconut plantations, beautiful rivers, houseboats, ayurvedic treatment and fish curries. The long coastline provides ample opportunity for fishing. Kerala's backwaters, wildlife sanctuaries, mountain ranges and beaches refresh your mind and body. Its unique culture and traditions have made Kerala one of the most popular tourist destinations in the world.

Kerala is known as the "Land of Spices". Most of the meals are cooked withcoconut oil, grated coconut, coconut milk and spices. Kerala cuisine is a blend of vegetarian and non-vegetarian dishes. It is known for hot and spicy food that is served on banana leaves. Rice and tapioca are staple foods and rice is the main dish of every meal. Eating rice with vegetables, fish, chicken or red meat curryis very common in Kerala.

Coconut oil, curry leaves, and coconut milk dominate the flavour of the traditional Kerala curries. Kerala curry or gravy is called Gassi. It's a traditional way of cooking fish in clay pots and most of the houses have at least one clay pot for making fish curry.

Appam with stew, is one of the traditional Kerala dishes. Appam, a thin pancake with crispy edges is made from fermented rice flour, coconut milk and coconut water. Stew is made with coconut milk and spices. 'Cappa meen curry' is a culinary tradition of Kerala. Cappa means tapioca and meen means fish. Spicy fish curry and steamed or mashed tapioca are a favourite preparation.

Ghee roast dosas, idlis, kerala style sambar, banana fritters, Malabar paratha, fish molee, spicy chicken fry, prawn curry, pumpkin and lentil stew, Iddiy appam, puttu and kadala curry are fondly eaten in all households in Kerala.

Payasam is a traditional Kerala Sweet made with Milk, grains, lentils and Jaggery or sugar. Grains like rice, broken wheat, millet, and semolina and Lentils like moong dal and chana dal are most commonly used to make payasam. Such delicious cuisine makes it a must-visit destination for travellers from all over the world.

Clay Pot Fish Curry (Mean Chatty Curry)

Ingredients : 250grams fish, cleaned and sliced, 2 ½ tbsp coconut oil, 1 onion, thinly sliced, 1 large tomato chopped, 8 fresh curry leaves, ½ tsp ginger-garlic paste, 2 ½ tsp chilli powder, 1 tsp coriander powder, ½ tsp turmeric powder, 2 medium kokum, 3/4th cup coconut milk. Salt as per taste.

Method : Soak kokum in water for 10 minutes. Rub fish pieces with salt and turmeric powder and keep covered for 15 minutes. Heat oil in a clay pot and fry onion for some time. Add tomatoes, curry leaves, ginger-garlic paste, chilli powder and coriander powder. Stir fry till oil separates. Add marinated fish and kokum water and cook till done. Finally, stir in coconut milk, and salt and simmer for 2 more minutes.

Serve hot with a bowl of steamed rice.

Vegetable Stew in Kerala Style

Ingredients : 1 large potato, 1 carrot, ½ cup green peas, 4 to 5 florets of cauliflower, 1 cup thick coconut milk, 1 tsp rice flour, 4 cloves, 2" piece cinnamon, 10 black peppercorns, 10 curry leaves, ½ tspsugar, 2 red chillies, salt to taste and 2 tbsp coconut oil.

Method : Peel and cut potato and carrot into cubes. Heat oil in a pan and splutter cloves, cinnamon, black peppercorns, curry leaves and chillies. Add vegetables and sauté. Add 1 cup of water and let the vegetables cook on low flame. Mix rice flour with coconut milk. When vegetables are almost done add coconut milk, salt and sugar. Simmer for 3 to 4 minutes. Serve hot with Rice or Appam.

Moong Dal Payasam (Paruppu Payasam)

Ingredients : ¾ cup moong dal, 1 tbsp ghee to roast moong dal, 1 cup jaggery, 1 cup coconut milk, 1 tsp ghee, 10 cashew nuts, a handful of raisins and 1 tbsp dry coconut slices. Pinch of cardamom powder.

Method : Fry cashew, raisins and coconut slices till golden brown. Take out and keep aside. Roast moong dal on low flame until it turns aromatic. Put roasted dal in a pressure cooker with water and remaining ghee. Pressure cook for 2 whistles or the dal turns soft. Dissolve jaggery in water and add to cooked moong dal. Boil the mixture for two minutes. Add cardamom powder and simmer for 2 minutes. Lastly, add thick coconut milk and mix well.

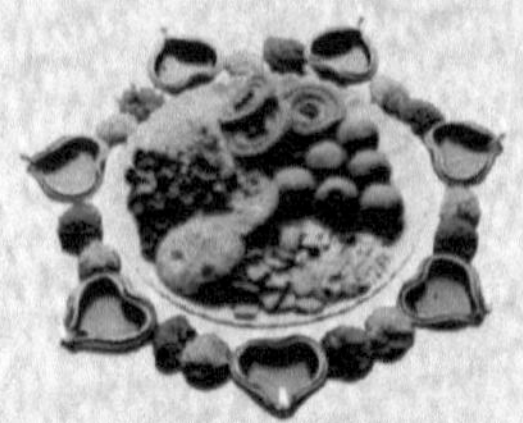

Interesting Facts About Indian Food

- India is a land of fasts, feasts and festivals.
- Indian cuisine is spicy, diverse and unique.
- Every Indian state has its special cuisine and style of preparation.
- Because of the cuisine-diverse country, there is no National dish of India until today.
- India is called the Land of Spices. No country in the world produces as many varieties of spices as India.
- Potato, tomato and chillies were brought to India by the Portuguese.
- Refined sugar was introduced to India by the Portuguese. Before that Fruits and honey were used as sweeteners in Indian food.
- Indian food has six different flavours : sweet, salty, bitter, sour, astringent and pungent. A proper Indian meal is a perfect balance of all six flavours, with one or two flavours standing out.
- Indian mealsare incomplete without side dishes like chutney and dal.
- Indians prepare a vast variety of Mithai and sweets. They are an important part of festivals and celebrations

Dining Etiquettes

The important characteristics of Indian Culture are hospitality, beliefs, values, etiquette, and rituals. The entire life of the Indian people is governed by the traditions and customs laid down by their ancestors and food is no exception. Inviting guests for food at home is a part of Indian hospitality. When invited for a meal in an Indian home, people may have a few questions in their mind. The dining etiquette varies a bit in different regions of India, but these facts will answer most of the questions.

- Always keep in mind that most Indians are very hospitable and love to entertain. It is a sign of honour and respect to ask somebody over for a meal.

- Don't be surprised if you casually visit an Indian friend and he/she asks you to stay over for a meal.

- It is quite okay to arrive at your host's place 15 to 20 minutes late. It is jokingly said as Indian Standard Time.

- After the meal is announced, you must wash and dry your hands. Washing your hands is the first step of dining as per Indian etiquette.

- Once the food is served it is customary to pray and then start eating. But that depends on your host.

- In India people mostly eat with their hands without using

any cutlery. Eating with the fingers is done neatly and only the tips of the fingers are used.

- The right hand is used for eating and the left hand is used for drinking water or passing dishes.
- It is perfectly acceptable for a guest to use cutlery to eat the meal.
- In most Indian homes, the lady of the house arranges food for the family on the table. She keeps an eye on who needs what and offers more food.
- All food is served in one go. The place on the plate to serve a particular dish is fixed.
- Indian culture highly encourages sharing food with others. If you're dining at an Indian restaurant and order different dishes, then it is customary to share your dish with the others.
- Saying 'take some more food' is the Indian way of showing love and respect.
- After the meal, you must compliment your host for the food. Since food is prepared with great effort and care, expressing your admiration will make the host happy.

India Special

One should be familiar with these words when in India.

Mud Chulha

Mud or clay chulha is a traditional earthen stove fueled by firewood or cow dung cakes. It is mostly used for indoor cooking. It is a U-shaped mud stove made from local clay. After the clay formation is complete it is  finished with a coat of clay and cow dunk mixture.

In the past, mud chulha used to be a significant part of Indian kitchens. People used to make it with their own hands. The mud chulha uses a slow cooking process so it keeps the minerals in the food intact. Food cooked in traditional chulha is lip-smacking and has a smoky flavour. There are villages in India, where people prefer food made on mud chulha as it is more flavour some.

Three-stone Stove

Three-stone stove is a traditional method used for outdoor cooking. It requires only three suitable stones of the same height on which a cooking pot is balanced over a fire. This is a very basic stove heated by burning wood.

This method of cooking is still used on farms. It is used for cooking as well as roasting potatoes, brinjal, sweet potato or onions. Chapati or Bhakri made on a stone stove becomes very tasty.

Kadhai

Kadhai is a cooking pan with a thick bottom, curved sides and handles. Indian kitchen is incomplete without a good Kadhai. Kadhais are made in a variety of materials, such as aluminium with non-stick finishing, stainless steel, cast iron, plain aluminium and so on.

Kadhai is a multi-purpose cooking pot which is used to make Indian curries, stew, stir-fried vegetables, deep-fried pakoras, samosas and many snacks.

Kadhai is the pride of every Indian kitchen.

Tadka Pot

Tadka pot, also known as a tempering pan or spice pan is an essential tool in the Indian kitchen. They are used to make flavourful and aromatic tadka. The tadka pot is a smaller version of kadhai with a long handle. The small size, depth and long handle of the tadka pot cater specifically for the tempering process.

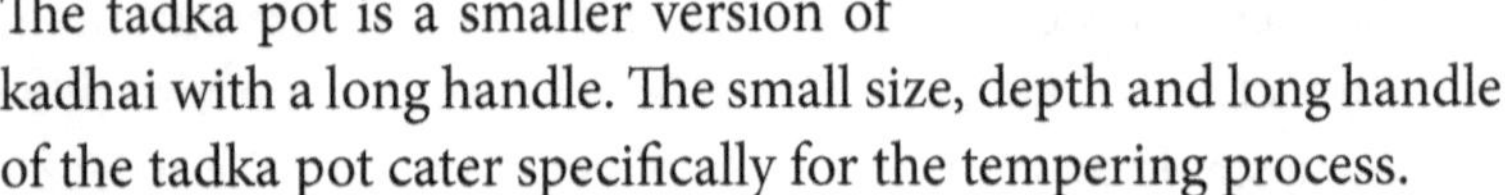

Kulhad

Kulhad is a traditional clay cup from ancient India. It is a handle-less clay cup that is used to serve hot beverages like tea, coffee or hot milk. They provide an earthy aroma to the beverage, which no other material can provide.

Kulhads are biodegradable and, hence can be thrown or broken after use. They are cheaper than plastic or glass containers. In India yoghurt, lassi and desserts like mishti doi, phirni and kulfi are also served in kulhads.

Masala Dabba

Masala Dabba is a circular spice box, often found in Indian homes. There are six to seven small containers for basic spices, inside the dabba. The spices included in the spice box vary from region to region. Common spices are cumin, mustard seeds, asafoetida, red chilli powder, turmeric powder and regional spice mix (masala).

Tiffin Carrier

Tiffin is a series of stacking containers and lids secured by a tension clip on the side. Each compartment can be filled with a separate food. The concept of carrying food from home to the workplace is very common in India. Usually, tiffin comes in three or four tiers. It is ideal for packinga variety of dishes like rice, salad, vegetables and dal or curry.

Dhaba

Dhaba means a roadside restaurant or roadside eateries in the state of Punjab. Dhabas, are a common feature on national and state highways. They are commonly found next to petrol stations and are open 24 hours a day.

Since many Indian truck drivers are of Punjabi origin, dhabas were earlier frequented only by truck drivers. Punjabi food is very popular throughout India so eating at a dhaba has become a trend. Today dhaba culture has become very popular among non-Punjabi people.

Mrinal Tulpule

Mrinal Tulpule has a bachelor's degree in Commerce and is a lawyer by profession. She has a diploma in Taxation law.

She has served in the Electronics and cardboard box Industry for thirty years.

Her hobbies include oil painting and travelling. She also loves to collect bells from various places. She has a collection of around 450 bells from different countries. Many of her interviews regarding this hobby are published in the Poona Herald, DNA, Sakal Times and Indian Express.

She has also written more than 900 articles for various publications like *Sakal, Saptahik Sakal, Tanishka, Maher, Pune Mirror, Mumbai Loksatta* and *Maharashtra Times.*

She has written and published ten books on Travel, Food and Coffee. Her first book '*Coffee Diary ani Pravas*' was awarded '*Smita Patil Sahitya Puraskar*'.

Tips :